TEACHING ICT THROUGH THE PRIMARY CURRICULUM

LEARNING
ICT
in the
HUMANITIES

Tony Pickford

David Fulton Publishers

David Fulton Publishers Ltd
The Chiswick Centre, 414 Chiswick High Road, London W4 5TF

www.fultonpublishers.co.uk

First published in Great Britain in 2006 by David Fulton Publishers

10 9 8 7 6 5 4 3 2 1

David Fulton Publishers is a division of Granada Learning Limited.

Copyright © Tony Pickford 2006

Note: The right of Tony Pickford to be identified as the author of this work has been asserted by him in accordance with the Copyright, Designs and Patents Act 1988.

British Library Cataloguing in Publication Data
A catalogue record for this book is available from the British Library.

ISBN: 1 84312 312 6 (EAN: 9781843123125)

Typeset by Servis Filmsetting Ltd, Manchester
Printed and bound in Great Britain

LEARNING
I.C.T
in the
HUMANITIES

University Centre at
Blackburn
College

Telephone: 01254 292165

Please return this book on or before the last date shown

Other titles in the Teaching ICT through the Primary Curriculum series:

Learning ICT in the Arts
Andrew Hamill
1-84312-313-4

Learning ICT with English
Richard Bennett
1-84312-309-6

Learning ICT with Maths
Richard Bennett
1-84312-310-X

Learning ICT with Science
Andrew Hamill
1-84312-311-8

Progression in Primary ICT
Richard Bennett, Andrew Hamill and Tony Pickford
1-84312-308-8

Contents

CD contents

Resources and links (MS Word)

Certificate Read-Me (Text file)

Coverage of ICT NC Programmes of Study by each project (MS Word)

Links to the QCA scheme of work for ICT in Key Stages 1 and 2 (MS Word)

Project 1

- Project 1 Completion Certificate (MS Word)
- Project 1 Completion 'Star' Certificate (MS Word)
- Project 1 Evaluation (MS Word)

Project 2

- Project 2 Completion Certificate (MS Word)
- Project 2 Completion 'Star' Certificate (MS Word)
- Local Studies Demo (Installation files)
- *Local Studies* booklet (MS Word)
- Project 2 Evaluation (MS Word)

Project 3

- Project 3 Completion Certificate (MS Word)
- Project 3 Completion 'Star' Certificate (MS Word)
- Project 3 Evaluation (MS Word)

Project 4

- Project 4 Completion Certificate (MS Word)
- Project 4 Completion 'Star' Certificate (MS Word)

- Example QuickTime VR files
- Key Stage 1 Project 4 Evaluation (MS Word)
- Key Stage 2 Project 4 Evaluation (MS Word)

Project 5

Project 5 Completion Certificate (MS Word)
Project 5 Completion 'Star' Certificate (MS Word)
Web browsing with Internet Explorer & Managing Favorites booklet (MS Word)
Project 5 Evaluation (MS Word)

Project 6

- Project 6 Completion Certificate (MS Word)
- Project 6 Completion 'Star' Certificate (MS Word)
- *Information Workshop* booklet (MS Word)
- 1881 Census data for Church Street, Chester: Information Workshop 2000 file (.IW2 file) and CSV file for import into other database software (.CSV file)
- 1901 Census data for Dig Lane, Padgate, Warrington, Cheshire: Information Workshop 2000 file (.IW2 file) and CSV file for import into other database software (.CSV file)
- Greenfield Road database activity (courtesy of MAPE – www.mape.org.uk) for Windows and Macintosh
- Project 6 Evaluation (MS Word)

Project 7

- Project 7 Completion Certificate (MS Word)
- Project 7 Completion 'Star' Certificate (MS Word)
- Project 7 Evaluation (MS Word)

Project 8

- Project 8 Completion Certificate (MS Word)
- Project 8 Completion 'Star' Certificate (MS Word)
- Time Lines Demo (Installation files)
- Project 8 Evaluation (MS Word)

Project 9

- Project 9 Completion Certificate (MS Word)
- Project 9 Completion 'Star' Certificate (MS Word)
- Project 9 Evaluation (MS Word)

Acknowledgements

The author would like to thank the following for their advice and help:

- Dr Carol Fry, subject leader for Religious Education in the School of Education at the University of Chester, for advice in relation to Project 4;

- Anna Bartholomew and Tony Ramsay of Soft Teach Educational, for preparation of the demo software on the CD-ROM;

- Bob Taylor, for many years of inspiration.

The author would like to thank the following for permission to reproduce screen images used in this publication:

- Adapt-IT

- Armchair Travel Co. Ltd

- RM plc

- Soft Teach Educational

- Softease Ltd

- Tiverton Museum Trust

- Yahoo! Media

- Black Cat (Granada Learning)

Introduction

This book is based on the belief that the integration of information and communication technology (ICT) and subject teaching is of benefit to children's development through the Foundation Stage, Key Stage 1 and Key Stage 2. It focuses on ICT in the context of three primary humanities subjects: geography, history and religious education. By incorporating some of the powerful ICT tools described in this book in your humanities planning, the quality of your teaching and children's learning will improve. Similarly, by contextualising the children's ICT experience in meaningful humanities projects, children's ICT capability will be enhanced and extended. *Learning ICT in the Humanities* is one of a series of ICT books: Teaching ICT through the Primary Curriculum. The core book for the series, *Progression in Primary ICT*, provides a more detailed discussion of the philosophy behind the approach and offers an overview and a planning matrix for all the projects described in the series.

The activities that are presented here offer practical guidance and suggestions for both teachers and trainees. For experienced teachers and practitioners there are ideas for ways that ICT can be developed through the areas of learning and primary humanities curriculum using ICT tools with which you are familiar. For less confident or less experienced users of ICT there are recommendations for resources and step-by-step guides aimed at developing your confidence and competence with ICT as you prepare the activities for your children.

The activities are related to the Foundation Stage areas of learning, the National Curriculum Programmes of Study (PoS) and the national framework for religious education. In some activities, such as Project 3: *Using an information source* and Project 6: *Using a database to analyse census data*, the emphasis is on finding things out with ICT. Other projects, e.g. Project 2: *Map making using GIS* and Project 9: *A video of a visit to a place of worship*, offer opportunities for developing ideas and making things happen using ICT tools. Children are provided with purposeful opportunities to exchange and share information in Project 5: *Repurposing information for different audiences* and Project 7: *Link with a contrasting locality*. Throughout all the projects, ways in which children can reflect on their use of ICT or explore its use in society are identified. Although the projects are clearly located in specified subject contexts, many could be easily adapted to other subjects.

The projects do not provide an exhaustive or definitive list of ICT opportunities in the humanities. Instead, they are tried and tested sequences of activities, adaptable across the age-range, which ensure that high quality learning in ICT is accompanied by high quality learning in a subject context. The projects are closely linked to relevant units in the Qualifications and Curriculum Authority (QCA) schemes of work for geography, history and religious education. They could be used to supplement, augment, extend or replace units in the ICT scheme of work. Although the projects are not future-proof, they have been designed to take advantage of some of the latest technologies now available in primary schools, such as interactive whiteboards, internet-linked computers and digital cameras.

A note on resources

Investment has improved the level of resources for the teaching of ICT in primary schools in recent years. The arrangement and availability of resources, however, still varies greatly from school to school. Some schools have invested heavily in centralised resources, setting up networked computer rooms or ICT suites. Some have gone down the route of networking the whole school, using wired or wireless technologies, with desktop or laptop computers being available in every classroom. Some schools have combined the two approaches, so that children have access to a networked suite and classroom computers. This book does not attempt to prescribe or promote a particular type of arrangement of computer hardware, but does make some assumptions in relation to the management of those resources. These assumptions are:

- ⊙ The teacher has access to a large computer display for software demonstration and the sharing of children's work – this could be in the form of an interactive whiteboard (IWB), a data projector and large screen or a large computer monitor.

- ⊙ Pupils (in groups or as individuals) have access to computers for hands-on activities – this may be in an ICT suite or by using a smaller number of classroom computers, perhaps on a rota basis.

- ⊙ The school has internet access, and at least one networked computer is linked to a large display, as described above.

- ⊙ Pupils have access to internet-linked computers and the school has a policy for safe use of the internet.

- ⊙ Teachers and pupils have access to a range of software packages, including a web browser, 'office' software (such as a word processor) and some 'educational' software. Although this book makes some recommendations with regard to appropriate software, it also suggests alternatives that could be used, if a specific a package is not available.

The projects

Each project is presented using the following format:

- a Fact Card which gives a brief overview of the project content and how it links to curriculum requirements and documentation;

- detailed guidance on how to teach a sequence of ICT activities in a subject context;

- information on pupils' prior learning required by the project;

- guidance for the teacher on the skills, knowledge and understanding required to teach the project, including step-by-step guidance on specific tasks, skills and tools;

- clear and specific information about what the children will learn in ICT and the subject;

- guidance on how to adapt the project for older or more experienced pupils;

- guidance on how to adapt the project for younger or less experienced pupils;

- a summary of reasons to teach the project, including reference to relevant curriculum documentation and research.

National Curriculum coverage

The ICT activities described in this book are those which are most relevant to Humanities learning and hence not all areas of the ICT curriculum have been covered. The core text for the series, *Progression in Primary ICT*, shows how coverage of the ICT curriculum can be achieved by selecting the most appropriate subject-related activities for your teaching situation and how progression in ICT capability can be accomplished through meaningful contexts. Figure 1 provides an indication of the aspects of ICT which are addressed by the projects in this book.

Focus age groups for each project

Figure 2 provides an indication of the age group for which each project has been written. However, most activities can be adapted for older or younger children and guidance on how this can be done is provided in the information for each project.

Coverage of ICT National Curriculum Programmes of Study by each project

Key Stage 1

Projects:	1	2	3	4	5	6	7	8	9
Finding things out									
1a. gather information from a variety of sources	✓		✓	✓					
1b. enter and store information in a variety of forms									
1c. retrieve information that has been stored			✓						
Developing ideas and making things happen									
2a. use text, tables, images and sound to develop their ideas		✓							
2b. select from and add to information they have retrieved for particular purposes									
2c. plan and give instructions to make things happen									
2d. try things out and explore what happens in real and imaginary situations	✓	✓	✓	✓					
Exchanging and sharing information									
3a. share their ideas by presenting information in a variety of forms		✓							
3b. present their completed work effectively		✓							

Key Stage 2

Projects:	1	2	3	4	5	6	7	8	9
Finding things out									
1a. talk about what information they need and how they can find and use it						✓		✓	
1b. prepare information for development using ICT, including selecting suitable sources, finding information, classifying it and checking it for accuracy					✓	✓		✓	
1c. interpret information, to check it is relevant and reasonable and to think about what might happen if there were any errors or omissions						✓			
Developing ideas and making things happen									
2a. develop and refine ideas by bringing together, organising and reorganising text, tables, images and sound as appropriate					✓			✓	✓
2b. create, test, improve and refine sequences of instructions to make things happen and to monitor events and respond to them									
2c. use simulations and explore models in order to answer 'What if … ?' questions, to investigate and evaluate the effect of changing values and to identify patterns and relationships									
Exchanging and sharing information									
3a. share and exchange information in a variety of forms, including e-mail							✓		✓
3b. be sensitive to the needs of the audience and think carefully about the content and quality when communicating information					✓		✓	✓	✓

Figure 1

Year groups covered by each project

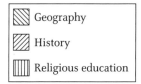

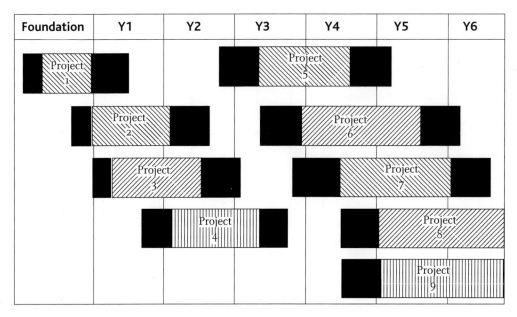

Figure 2

Links to the QCA scheme of work for ICT

Figure 3 indicates the relationship between the projects included in this book and the QCA ICT units in Key Stages 1 and 2. QCA scheme of work units that can be replaced by one of the projects are marked ▨. Where a partial covering of the learning described in a unit is addressed by a project, ▨ signifies the supporting role played by the project. The activities outlined in projects so marked could be used to revisit or reinforce learning. ▥ suggests units where a project provides a greater challenge and extends the learning potential described in the scheme of work.

Links to the QCA scheme of work for ICT in Key Stages 1 and 2

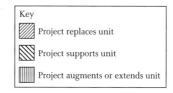

Key
- ▨ Project replaces unit
- ▧ Project supports unit
- ▥ Project augments or extends unit

Projects:	1	2	3	4	5	6	7	8	9
Unit 1A: An introduction to modelling	replaces	augments							
Unit 1C: The information around us	supports		augments						
Unit 2B: Creating pictures	supports	replaces							
Unit 2C: Finding information			augments	augments					
Unit 2E: Questions and answers				augments					
Unit 3E: E-mail							replaces		
Unit 4A: Writing for different audiences					replaces		augments		
Unit 4D: Collecting and presenting information: questionnaires and pie charts						augments			
Unit 5B: Analysing data and asking questions: using a complex searches						replaces			
Unit 5C: Evaluating information, checking accuracy and questioning plausibility						augments			
Unit 6A: Multimedia presentation							replaces	supports	
Unit 6D: Using the internet to search large databases and to interpret information							supports		

Figure 3

GEOGRAPHY/SENSE OF PLACE

Project Fact Card: Project 1: Decision making with a mouse

Who is it for?

- 4– to 6-year-olds (Working towards NC Levels 1–2)

What will the children do?

Pupils will explore and interact with decision-making games on a website, using a simple input device, e.g. a mouse. They will select options by clicking a button and/or by dragging and dropping. They will recognise that the choices they make will lead to different outcomes and the computer can give feedback. In the context of the subject, they will make observations about where things are located and recognise changes in an environment.

What do I need to know?

- The URLs of the BBC Schools website (www.bbc.co.uk/schools) and the BBC Barnaby Bear website (www.bbc.co.uk/schools/barnabybear)
- Appropriate geographical vocabulary to describe features in an environment

What resources will I need?

- A web browser, e.g. Microsoft *Internet Explorer* or Mozilla *Firefox*

What should the children know already?

- That a mouse can be used to control a pointer on screen
- They can follow simple spoken instructions, given by a computer
- That certain objects and features can be found in specific localities, e.g. a cow on a farm, a deckchair on a beach

What will the children learn?

- How to control effects and actions on screen using mouse functions, e.g. clicking a mouse button, dragging and dropping
- That a computer representation allows the user to make choices and that different decisions produce different outcomes

How to challenge the more able

- Move the pupils on to more challenging games on the BBC Barnaby Bear website – these may be more advanced in terms of ICT skill requirements and/or geographical content

How to support the less able

- Provide support from a teaching assistant or other helper
- Use an input device which requires fewer fine motor skills, e.g. a large trackball

Why teach this?

- The project provides scope for children to demonstrate key aspects of the early learning goal for ICT in *Curriculum Guidance for the Foundation Stage*, specifically that they 'complete a simple program' on the computer. It provides an opportunity for an early years practitioner to develop skills across the areas of learning, especially in relation to sense of place.
- The project also provides a seamless link to ICT NC KS1 PoS statements 1a and 2d.
- The project supports the content of QCA ICT Scheme of Work Units 1A, 1C and 2B. It also supports Geography Scheme of Work Unit 5: *Where in the world is Barnaby Bear?*

Decision making with a mouse

What will the children do?

Children coming into Foundation Stage settings will have a range of basic computer skills. Some will be quite sophisticated users of PC input devices, such as mouse and keyboard. Others will have had little or no experience of computers, but may be familiar with games consoles and their keypads. A few children will have had no experience of interactive electronic devices of any kind. Relatively simple 'games' such as those on the BBC Barnaby Bear website – www.bbc.co.uk/schools/barnabybear – provide a means by which pupils from a range of backgrounds can acquire and/or practise 'mouse skills' in a purposeful way. More skilled pupils will be able to focus on the geographical content more readily and can be moved on to use their skills in other contexts within the site. Children who are less familiar with the mouse and its functions will gain competence/confidence by performing relatively simple tasks and will be supported by positive feedback from the Barnaby Bear character.

Activity 1: Introducing the Barnaby Bear website

Prior to the first ICT-based activity, children should be introduced to the character of Barnaby Bear and his travels. The original idea, on which Geography Scheme of Work Unit 5 is based, is that Barnaby is a teddy bear soft toy, which accompanies adults (teachers, parents, governors) and children whenever they visit places away from the school's local area. Barnaby is photographed in these new places and sends back postcards to the children describing what he has seen and done. Although a Barnaby Bear soft toy puppet can be purchased from the Geographical Association (www.geographyshop.org.uk), any teddy bear can be used as 'a first-hand object' to give children a sense of personal involvement in visits to distant localities. Barnaby now also features in a range of books published by the Geographical Association (www.geography.org.uk) and is the subject of a BBC Schools television series (www.bbc.co.uk/schools). The Barnaby Bear website is an offshoot of the latter series and contains a set of related activities. It is not reliant on the series, however, and providing children are familiar with the character, the activities can be carried out independently.

After introducing the Barnaby Bear character, preferably in the form of a soft toy that is familiar to the children, explain to them that they are going to carry out an activity on the computer. Gather children (either the whole class or a group) so that they can see the website on a large screen. Show the site's home page, with its picture of Barnaby and a suitcase – then, using either the link on one of the suitcase's labels or the link on the left of the screen, go to the 'Games' section of the site. Discuss with the children what can be seen on screen. Point out the link to the 'Out of Place' game and click on it – select the Full Screen mode for the game. Ask the children to listen carefully and then let Barnaby explain the activity on screen. Explain to the children that when they come to do the activity on their own or in groups, the game will have been located for them and they will not need to navigate through the site.

Check that the children understand the task. They have to identify features and objects which are 'out of place' in two settings – an airport and a beach. They then have to move the objects to the correct location by dragging and dropping. Demonstrate how this is done – click and hold down the left mouse button when the mouse pointer is over an object, then move the pointer and object across the screen. When an object has been moved to the correct setting, releasing the mouse button makes it jump into place with a satisfying 'boing' sound. When all objects have been moved successfully, the Barnaby character gives positive feedback, in the form of on-screen text and speech. Ask selected children to come out to the computer and try the task. Explain that when they have placed all the objects in the correct settings, there is a second game that you want them to try, in which misplaced objects must be moved between a classroom and a farm.

The second pair of environments in the 'Out of Place' game – a classroom and a farm

Depending on the size of the group, it may be possible to use this introductory activity as a means of assessing the children's mouse skills or you may already have a fair idea of their skills from previous experience of their work or play on the computer. Stress to the children that, when they come to do the activity independently, they must take turns in using the mouse and also talk to each other about the objects they move and why.

Activity 2: Dragging and dropping

Children can either work through the 'Out of Place' game individually, in pairs or with the help of a teaching assistant. Groupings will depend very much on your professional judgement of children's abilities. Working in pairs is the preferable option, as it will allow you to group children so that the more experienced/ confident mouse users can support the less skilled (without, of course, dominating and taking over). Pairings of children will also provide a context for exploratory talk (for more information, see *Learning ICT in English* Project 3). You may use a teaching assistant to help the least skilled mouse users and/or to prompt discussion about the objects and the settings.

Monitoring of children's performance will help you decide how to move them on. Further practice in dragging and dropping on-screen objects could be gained by working through the 'Weather Report' and 'Recycling' games. Children needing practice in selecting and clicking on objects could work through the 'What's Changed?' activity. Although the mouse skills required by these are relatively easy, they are more demanding in terms of geographical understandings and knowledge.

When all the children have completed the two stages of the 'Out of Place' game, gather them together for a plenary. Ask them to describe the different environments in the game. Ask individuals to explain why they moved objects from one setting to another. How did they know that they were right in their choices of objects? Make the point that the computer and mouse made their decision making easier, because they quickly knew if they were right or wrong. Ask children who have moved on to other games to describe what they did. Did they use the mouse in the same or in different ways?

Activity 3: Stories about Barnaby Bear

The third activity from the Barnaby Bear website could be carried out as a whole-class activity or as a small-group task with pairs of children working co-operatively. The 'Stories' section of the website contains two stories in the form of talking books – 'Barnaby Down Under' and 'Barnaby's Day Trip to Paris'. The latter is probably most suitable for younger children.

A storyteller narrates the story through a series of linked, animated screens. Clicking on right and left arrows at the foot of the screen moves the story forward or backward and, on some screens, there is a mouse symbol which, when clicked, leads to further animations and effects. On most of the screens, Barnaby and other characters in the story 'speak' to the children, with their words shown in speech bubbles for more able readers.

Clicking on the mouse symbol on this screen starts an animation showing a lift ascending the Eiffel Tower

At the most basic level, the story gives scope for the practising of point and click mouse skills. Once again, children will have to make decisions about which symbols to click and, to an extent, the order in which the story is viewed. Although linear in structure, children can move backwards as well as forwards through the story, revisiting favourite parts if they wish.

The geographical content of the story will be challenging for young children. It involves a journey by 'Eurostar' train and a brief tour around some Paris sites. The level of challenge is mitigated, however, by the presence of the familiar Barnaby Bear character. Liz, another character, also makes the story more accessible by explaining events and describing features in relatively simple terms. There are a great many opportunities to make comparisons between Paris and the local area and also between Barnaby's journey and journeys the children have experienced.

What should the children know already?

Children need to have had some experience of the basic point and click functions of a mouse before embarking on this project. They also should have some experience of listening to voice instructions from a computer. Many software applications intended for an early years audience provide voice instructions and feedback, e.g. *Fizzy's First Numbers* or *Tizzy's Toybox*, published by Sherston software. Such packages are suitable for group or individual use and will help to develop appropriate listening skills. Although the project provides a context for the introduction of the skill of dragging and dropping on-screen objects with a mouse, children may benefit from having had previous experience. *My World* (published by Inclusive

Technology – www.inclusive.co.uk) is probably the most familiar software tool for developing this skill.

The 'Out of Place' game that is the focus of this project requires relatively simple ICT skills, but has geographical content that some children may find quite challenging. It requires some familiarity with the characteristics of four environments – a beach, an airport, a farm and a classroom. Although familiarity with the last of these should be easy to facilitate, the others may require some initial preparation. This could be done through class/group discussion of images or by sharing the first-hand experience of children or adults who have visited these places.

To get the most from Activity 3, children should have some familiarity with the features of their local area, so that they can make comparisons with the Parisian localities visited by Barnaby. You could also get children to talk about any long journeys they have made and how they have travelled to places beyond the local area.

What do I need to know?

The URLs (Uniform Resource Locators) of the BBC Schools website and the BBC Barnaby Bear website

As one would expect for such a simple first project, the ICT skills demanded of the teacher are relatively straightforward. You will need to know how to show a website on an interactive whiteboard or large screen and how to drag and drop on-screen objects using a mouse. You will need to be familiar with the structure and layout of the BBC Barnaby Bear website (www.bbc.co.uk/schools/barnabybear). The structure is relatively simple with all sections being accessible from the initial screen. There is a comprehensive 'Teachers and Parents' section, which provides an introduction to the site, useful web links and an overview of National Curriculum coverage for each of the sections.

If it is difficult to link a networked computer to an interactive whiteboard or large screen, you may wish to download the Barnaby Bear website to a computer's hard disk and then transfer it to your classroom computer. This will involve the use of offline browsing software. This is discussed in more detail in Project 4.

Appropriate geographical vocabulary to describe features in an environment

The geographical understandings demanded by the project are similarly straightforward. You will need to introduce children to appropriate language to describe the locations in the 'Out of Place' game and also language to express opinions about the features of their own and contrasting locations. The 'sense of place' early learning goal in *Curriculum Guidance for the Foundation Stage* suggests the following list of words: 'busy', 'quiet', 'noisy', 'attractive', 'ugly', 'litter', 'pollution'. The specific locations in the 'Out of Place' screens may be quite unfamiliar, so you may have to introduce several 'new' words to the children – the airport screen, in particular, will be challenging for children who have never travelled by air or seen an airport on television or in a film.

What will the children learn?

The key ICT skill that children will learn from the main activity in this project is how to drag and drop objects on screen. At the level of key ideas, they will learn that a computer representation allows the user to make choices and that different decisions produce different outcomes. Although these outcomes are relatively limited (the successful movement of objects and, in Activity 3, the activation of animations), the activities make the key point that the children can control the computer, rather than the other way round. This is a key point to be raised in a plenary at the end of the project.

Challenging the more able and supporting the less able: modifying the project for older and younger pupils

More experienced or older pupils could move on to more challenging games on the BBC Barnaby Bear website. Most are not more sophisticated in terms of ICT skills, but have more demanding geographical content. 'The Recycling Game', for example, involves dragging and dropping different objects into recycling containers, according to the materials they are made from. The activity could link well to recycling initiatives in the school or in the local area.

'What's Changed?' is demanding in terms of the required historical understandings – children have to identify aspects of a countryside scene that would have been different 100 years ago. The Barnaby character gives detailed spoken explanations for each of the changes, but further explanation by yourself or a teaching assistant may also be needed. Of the other games on the site, 'Weather Report' is most suitable for younger children, but still requires quite advanced reading skills, as the task is to place weather symbols on particular locations on a UK map.

Children with limited experience or less well-developed skills will need support from a teaching assistant or other helper, at least, when first beginning to carry out Activity 2 independently. This help should focus on showing how to drag and drop and not on doing the activity for the children. Children soon acquire the skill, but tend to find the double task of holding down the mouse button while moving the mouse initially quite difficult. Overcoming any initial frustration, with praise and hands-on support, is vital.

Children whose fine motor skills are less well developed could benefit from the use of an alternative input device, such as a large trackball as shown.

'Big Track' – a large trackball for children with less well-developed fine motor skills (available from Adapt-IT – www.adapt-it.org.uk)

Why teach this?

As well as helping to meet Foundation Stage goals for ICT, the project provides a link to the 'Developing ideas and making things happen' strand of the National Curriculum requirements at Key Stage 1, in that it enables children to 'try things out and explore what happens in real and imaginary situations' (PoS 2d). The geographical content also serves to provide a link between the relatively parochial requirements of the Foundation Stage curriculum and the National Curriculum's wider perspective on contrasting locations. Pupils will 'notice differences' and 'observe, find out about and identify features' in an environment, as required by the 'sense of place' early learning goal. As the environment in question is not within the school's locality, it extends the children's range of geographical experiences and links to Geography National Curriculum programme of study requirements – specifically, 3d: 'recognise how places compare with other places'.

The project supports the content of QCA ICT Scheme of Work Units 1A: *An introduction to modelling*, 1c: *The infomation around us* and 2B: *Creating pictures*, by giving an opportunity to develop essential prerequisite skills and by giving experience of decision making within visual, web-based environments. It also supports Geography Scheme of Work Unit 5: *Where in the world is Barnaby Bear?* – an ongoing, 'continuous' unit within the scheme which aims to introduce children to contrasting places through the character of Barnaby Bear. As the unit is intended to feature throughout Key Stage 1, it is appropriate that children should be introduced to Barnaby and his travels in the Foundation Stage.

Although some researchers argue that exposure to computer-based activities in the Foundation Stage may be counter-productive, e.g. Healy (1998), many others suggest that well-chosen software accompanied by appropriate teacher intervention can have a positive effect on children's learning (Stephen and Plowman 2002). The acquisition of skills, such as dragging and dropping, will increase children's independence and enable them to move on from the simple, point-and-click, drill-and-practice programs that are often found in early years settings. Use of multimedia websites, such as the BBC Barnaby Bear site (www.bbc.co.uk/schools/barnaby bear), will also contribute to the development of children's multimedia literacy, including 'familiarity with screen conventions and how to map icons onto actions and screen events' (ibid.). The project provides an enriching experience which paves the way for later projects which will use the newly developed skills in a range of contexts.

See *Learning ICT with Science* Project 1 (Drag and drop sorting) and *Arts* Project 1 (Building pictures) for related activities.

References and further reading

Healy, J. (1998) *Failure to Connect: How Computers Affect Our Children's Minds – For Better or Worse?* New York: Simon & Schuster.

QCA (2000) *Curriculum Guidance for the Foundation Stage*. London: QCA.

Stephen, C. and Plowman, L. (2002) *ICT in Pre-school: A 'Benign Addition'? A review of the literature on ICT in pre-school settings*. Edinburgh: Learning and Teaching Scotland.

GEOGRAPHY/SENSE OF PLACE

Project Fact Card: Project 2: Map making using GIS

Who is it for?

- 5- to 7-year-olds (NC Levels 1–3)

What do I need to know?

- The functions and features of a simple Geographical Information System (GIS) program, e.g. *Local Studies*

What will the children do?

Following fieldwork in the locality, e.g. a walk focusing on features such as shops, services, jobs, etc., pupils use map-making software to create a simple map, recording the route and the features that have been observed.

What resources will I need?

- A simple GIS program, e.g. *Local Studies* or *Easiteach Geography Map Builder*

What should the children know already?

- That a mouse can be used to make 'marks' on screen in the form of lines and fills of different colours
- How to move items around on screen using drag and drop

What will the children learn?

- That ICT can be used to create pictures of different types, including map representations
- That effective maps use agreed or standardised symbols and ICT makes map making easier
- That ICT makes it easy to correct mistakes and explore alternatives

How to challenge the more able

- More able and/or older pupils could use more advanced functions of the GIS program, e.g. adding additional information about features or using more abstract symbols
- They could be encouraged to make more detailed comparisons between hand-drawn and computer-drawn maps

How to support the less able

- Younger children and/or less able pupils could be given more time to play with the features of the GIS program before being required to make a map of the locality
- They could be given more time and/or more adult support to enable them to complete their map
- They could be provided with a partially completed map on which to add additional features

Why teach this?

- The project is targeted on ICT NC KS1 PoS statements 2a, 2d, 3a and 3b.
- The project augments and extends the content of QCA ICT Scheme of Work Units 1A and 2B. It provides highly appropriate ICT content for QCA Geography Scheme of Work Unit 1: *Around our school – the local area.*

Map making using GIS

What will the children do?

Since a key geographical purpose of the project is to highlight the importance of using a shared set of map symbols, so that everyone understands each other's maps, children should create maps of an agreed route, not a disparate set of routes to school. Before doing the first activity, take the children for a short walk around a chosen route in the locality making a note of key features. Ask them to produce a hand-drawn map of the shared route. The walk around the locality will obviously require some pre-planning, e.g. parental permission will need to gained, adult helpers will need to be recruited and briefed, clipboards and pens will need to be organised. Although the route could take in a random set of notable features (e.g. a local parade of shops, a church, a factory, a busy road), a theme could give the walk more purpose, e.g. children could be asked to record places where people work or places of worship or places that they like and/or dislike in the locality. Recording while on the walk could take different forms – some children could draw features, others record in written note form, others record spoken notes into a small tape or digital recorder, others take photographs. As small digital video cameras are now relatively inexpensive and user-friendly, they provide another means of recording, although they are perhaps better in the hands of a teacher or other adult helper.

Follow the making of hand-drawn maps with a plenary. Firstly, children will need to be reminded about the nature of maps and how they differ from 'pictures'. Maps of different types and at different scales should be a permanent feature of classroom displays and children should have gained practical, kinaesthetic experience of laminated play maps and play mats in free play contexts. They will need to be reminded that maps take an objective 'plan view' of a place from a viewpoint that is vertically above. Secondly, they will need to be reminded about the route that they have walked, in terms of the sequence of features observed. You could do this through focused questioning or by use of the children's sketches, photographs or video clips. Emphasise to the children that recording of the sequence of features is the key purpose of the task, not an absolute accuracy of 'plan-view'. Also emphasise that the maps need to be clear and understandable to an outsider, so that the same route could be followed – the character of Barnaby Bear could come in useful here, as a potential audience.

Children are often introduced to the idea that they can make maps by being asked to create a map of their route to school. This is a perfectly legitimate activity in that it will focus attention on features of the local area that pupils see every day and encourage them to take a projective view of their locality. For this ICT project, a map of the route to school is not an ideal context for two reasons: (a) as children live in different places relative to the school, the maps they will produce will be different, not just in terms of graphic skills, but also in terms of content, distance and direction; (b) as children travel to school in different ways (e.g. by car, on foot, by taxi, etc.) they will not have an equal opportunity to note the features seen *en route*.

Activity 1: Introducing map symbols

When the children have completed their hand-drawn maps, working individually and independently, gather them together for a plenary. Get the children to share their maps – perhaps by putting them on a wall display or by asking children to come to the front of the room in groups to hold them up. Focus comments and questioning on the different ways children have represented a key feature, e.g. a mosque, a farm or a shop. Raise the questions: 'How could we make sure that everyone (or Barnaby) understands all the maps?' and/or 'How could we make sure that everyone (or Barnaby) understands which is the mosque/farm/shop?'

Make the point that if everyone used the same picture (symbol), the maps could be understood by anyone. Using a conventional whiteboard and marker or similar, get selected children to draw their representations for a chosen feature. Using a simple 'hands up' vote, decide which representation is the 'best' symbol for a chosen feature and show how it can be explained using a key, e.g. 'symbol' = Mosque/farm/shop. Explain that the chosen representation is now our chosen symbol for the feature. It would be a very time-consuming process to get children to select symbols for all the features of a locality in the same way, but this would be a necessary precursor to drawing a second set of maps with 'agreed' symbols.

Make sure all the children can see the chosen GIS program. Point out the symbols used by the program to represent features found in the locality. Show the children how the symbols can be placed on the screen. Emphasise that, because the program uses an 'agreed' set of symbols, we will all be able to understand maps made using the program. Make a link to the symbol or symbols chosen by the children for a feature or features in the locality.

Explain that you want the children to work, either individually or in small groups, to produce a map of the locality using the GIS program. Stress that they should try to make the map as accurate as possible and use the symbols in the program to represent the features in the locality that they saw on the walk. Explain that if they cannot find a specific symbol for a particular feature, they should choose the 'best' symbol in the set to represent it. Finally, explain that you want children to use only the painting tools (lines) and the symbols to create their maps.

Activity 2: Using map symbols

Depending on available resources, pupils should now work individually or in groups on their maps using the GIS program. Small groups of two or three children are, probably, ideal as co-operative work on a map will foster discussion and exploratory talk about maps, symbols and the chosen features of the locality. Well-chosen groups will also provide support for less confident pupils – it is important to emphasise that the map-making process should be shared between group members, with no one person dominating. Appropriate interactions by yourself, or a teaching assistant, should focus on ensuring that all children gain experience of working with the program.

At the end of this activity, a range of maps should be printed or saved to a shared network drive so that they can be viewed by the whole class on a large screen. Focus your plenary on identifying differences between the hand-drawn and computer-based maps. Focus in particular on the symbols used on the maps made using the GIS program. A key question will be: 'Would a stranger to the locality (or Barnaby) find these maps easier to understand? Why?'

Activity 3: Adding labels

In this activity, explain that you want the children to do some further work on their computer-based maps. Show the children a selection of published maps, e.g. a local town plan, a large-scale Ordnance Survey (OS) map, an A–Z map, and ask them to identify any differences between their maps and the published maps. Through discussion, identify the key point that, as well as lines and symbols, most maps also contain labels in the form of simple text. Explain that you want the children to add some labels to their maps using the GIS program. Demonstrate how to add labels to a map on screen using the program's Text tool.

Set an achievable target for the class, or groups within it – e.g. labels for four or six or eight features – and set the children to work in groups. For this activity, group working (and support from a teaching assistant) will be essential to provide support for the less able readers and writers.

In a plenary, at the end of the activity, show a sample of finished maps (either printed or on screen) and ask children to identify the key elements of a map. Through prompting, questioning and discussion, the children should recognise that maps convey information using coloured lines (and fills), standardised symbols and labels. Finally, ask children to compare the process of drawing maps by hand and using a simple GIS program. Key questions will include:

⊙ Which type of map making did you prefer? Why?

⊙ Which type of map making allowed mistakes to be corrected more easily?

⊙ Which maps (hand-drawn or computer-based) would a visitor to the locality (or Barnaby) be able to 'read' more easily?

What should the children know already?

Depending to an extent on the chosen GIS program, children will need to bring a range of skills to this project. They will need to know that a mouse (or other input device, e.g. a large trackball) can be used to make 'marks' on screen in the form of lines and fills of different colours. They will need to know how to move items around on screen using drag and drop (see Project 1). It would be useful, but not essential, for children to have had some experience of making images using a computer-based painting program, e.g. *Microsoft Paint* for Windows.

What do I need to know?

The functions and features of a simple GIS program, e.g. *Local Studies*

To confidently teach this project, you will need to know the basic functions of a chosen GIS program. GIS stands for 'Geographical Information System' and is a shorthand term for software that enables maps to be stored, retrieved, analysed and annotated. High end GIS programs used by professionals, such as academic geographers and planners, can be expensive and have demanding hardware requirements. Fortunately, there are some GIS programs available which have simple user interfaces and will easily run on school computers. Two examples are *Local Studies* (published by Soft Teach – www.soft-teach.co.uk) and *Easiteach Geography Map Builder* (part of *Easiteach Primary Geography*, published by RM plc (RM) – www.rm.com/primary). Both feature tools for creating simple maps made up of coloured lines, symbols and text labels. The approaches taken by the two programs are slightly different, but the results, in terms of printed or on-screen maps, are very similar.

A demo of *Local Studies* is available on the CD.

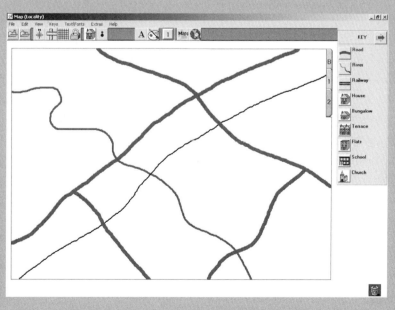

A simple map created using only the line tools in Local Studies

Local Studies is the longer-established of the two programs. It is available for Windows and Macintosh, providing a very similar user interface on both platforms. On starting the program, the user is presented with a simple interface, consisting of a large blank area for map creation and toolbars at the top and right-hand side of the screen.

In *Local Studies*, the toolbar on the right is the most important for this project as it contains the painting tools and symbols for the map. Clicking on the **Road**, **River** and **Railway** buttons on the toolbar enables the user to draw red (Road), blue (River or waterway) or black (Railway) lines on screen using the mouse pointer.

Symbols can then be added by dragging and dropping the icons onto the map screen. Lines can be erased and changed using an **Eraser** tool in the **Text/Fonts** menu. Misplaced icons can be discarded by dragging and dropping them to the **Bin** icon at the bottom-right of the program window. Further symbols can be accessed by clicking on the arrow at the top of the right-hand toolbar.

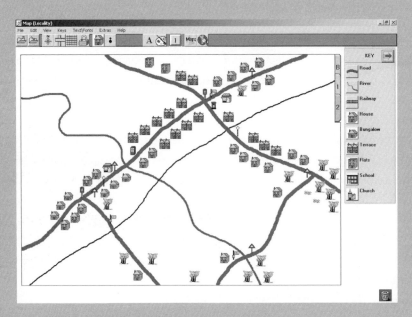

A simple map created using the line and symbol tools in Local Studies

Although an additional set of symbols is available (accessed from the **Keys** menu), the basic set should be sufficient for this project. Labels can be added to the map using the **Text** button in the toolbar at the top of the screen ⒜. Click on the button and an outline box appears that can be moved around the map using the mouse pointer. Once text has been entered, double clicking on the box locks it into position.

Local Studies provides a range of printing options. A map can be printed at A4 size or a complete 'project' can be printed as a booklet with a title page, a map and a complete key for all the lines and symbols used.

Easiteach Geography Map Builder is accessed from the **Geography** toolbar in *Easiteach*. A floating toolbar appears which contains the map components – road, path, waterway and railway drawing tools are at the top and a scrolling box containing symbols for a range of features is at the bottom of the toolbar. Under each set of components are rows of three buttons, which are used to select the size of the lines or symbols to be inserted into the map.

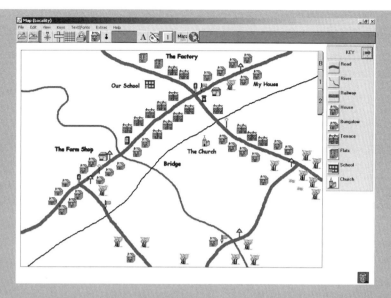

A simple map created using the line, symbol and text tools in Local Studies

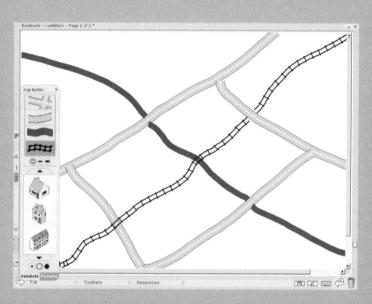

A simple map created using only the line tools in Easiteach Geography Map Builder

In the screenshot above, the left-hand buttons have been selected, indicating that the lines and symbols will be at the smallest setting.

Both lines and symbols are placed on the map in the same way as in *Local Studies*. After clicking on the desired type of line in the toolbar (road, path, waterway or railway), the mouse pointer becomes a drawing tool. Holding down the left mouse button while moving the mouse leaves a line of the desired type on screen. Symbols are moved from the toolbar to the map by drag and drop. Deleting items is a more complicated procedure than in *Local Studies*. The screen must be switched from 'Use Mode' to 'Edit Mode' in the *Easiteach* toolbar – see the image overleaf. An item (line or symbol) can then be deleted by double clicking with the left mouse button when the mouse pointer is over it to select and pressing the DELETE (Del) or BACKSPACE (←) key on the keyboard.

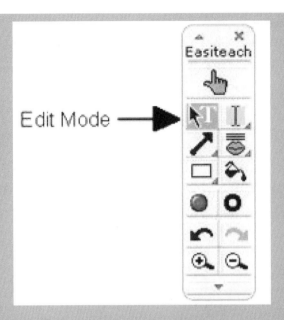

The Easiteach *toolbar*

Map Builder has a much wider range of symbols than *Local Studies* – there are, for example, symbols of places of worship for four major religions, not just a Christian church – and the line tools create more 'realistic' roads, paths and railway lines. Both programs contain symbols, which are oblique, rather than plan views of objects and features. This may be seen as a disadvantage of computer-based map making as the crucial concept of a map as a plan or 'bird's eye' view is not reinforced by the programs. This disadvantage is far outweighed by the advantages, however, especially the facility to use standardised symbols and the support offered to children with less well-developed drawing skills. As in *Local Studies*, an additional set of OS style symbols can be accessed by clicking on the **Symbols** tab at the foot of the *Map Builder* toolbar.

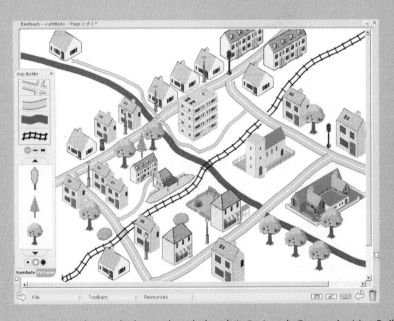

A simple map created using the line and symbol tools in Easiteach Geography Map Builder

Text labels can be added to the map in *Map Builder* very easily. When in 'Edit Mode', the user can click anywhere on screen and type appropriate text. The map screen can be printed easily, but there is no facility to print a key of symbols used in *Map Builder*.

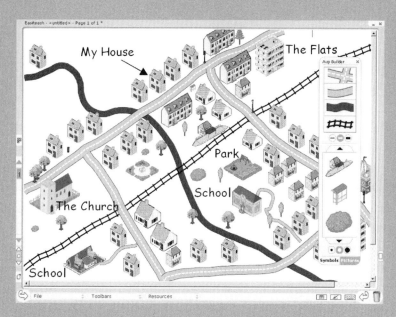

A simple map created using the line, symbol and text tools in
Easiteach Geography Map Builder

What will the children learn?

The project helps children gain competence and confidence in the use of content-free software. They will learn that ICT can be used to create map representations and that ICT makes it easy to correct mistakes and explore alternatives. They will learn to select and use different tools (lines, symbols, text) to communicate ideas through maps.

The project encourages children to take a projective (or objective) view of their locality and consider what features to include in a map. It will develop understandings about the nature of map representations, particularly about the importance of using agreed or standardised symbols to communicate meaning clearly to an audience. The project will facilitate discussion about features of the locality and begin to foster an understanding of the character of the place where the children live. In common with QCA Primary Geography Scheme of Work Unit 1, children will learn 'to describe a route', 'to recognise physical and human features in their locality' and 'to identify some of the uses of land and buildings in their locality'.

To an extent, children's learning will be affected by the choice of map-making program used in the project. *Map Builder* produces map representations that are less stylised and abstract than those produced by *Local Studies*. For this reason it could be argued that children will learn less about map conventions because essentially they are producing an oblique-angled 'picture'. *Map Builder* is more demanding in terms of ICT skills, however, in that children have to cope with a floating toolbar that can be moved around the screen. Although the lines and symbols in *Local Studies* are less realistic than in *Map Builder*, the ICT skills required to produce a map are less demanding – the toolbars are fixed and erasing features is a much more straightforward process.

Challenging the more able and supporting the less able: modifying the project for older and younger pupils

More experienced and/or older pupils could use the more advanced functions of the chosen GIS program, e.g. in *Local Studies* they could add additional information about features using the 'Hotspots' facility or use symbols from one of the additional keys; in *Map Builder* they could be encouraged to use the OS style symbols. Alternatively, your questioning could encourage more detailed comparisons between the hand-drawn and computer-drawn maps. Questions like 'Which maps are more accurate?' or 'Which maps look more like our locality?' should enable children to address more advanced ideas in the 'Reviewing, modifying and evaluating work as it progresses' strand of ICT in the National Curriculum – they will begin to compare different methods of completing a task and the needs of an audience.

Younger children and/or less experienced pupils could be given more time to 'play' with the features of the GIS program before being required to make a map of the locality. Both *Local Studies* and *Map Builder* are essentially painting programs, with subject-specific tools, and children with little experience of picture-making software will need time to explore functions and features. Relatively free play, without the limitations of a specific task to complete, will build both competence and confidence with the software. Less experienced pupils would benefit from additional adult support when working with GIS. More time would also be beneficial, as would a partially completed map, to get over any initial problems caused by the large, intimidating white space of a blank map-making screen.

Why teach this?

The project augments and extends the content of QCA ICT Scheme of Work Units 1A: *An introduction to modelling* and 2B: *Creating pictures*, by providing an additional context for the exploration of alternatives and the communication of visual information. It provides highly appropriate ICT content for QCA Geography Scheme of Work Unit 1: *Around our school – the local area* and, if the chosen theme for the children's maps is road safety, it could provide an effective ICT link within Unit 2: *How can we make our local area safer?*

The project addresses key requirements in the 'Developing ideas and making things happen' strand of ICT in the National Curriculum at Key Stage 1. It provides a particularly appropriate context for children to try things out, make changes and explore alternatives. Mistakes and errors, which would pose serious problems when drawing a map by hand, can be easily corrected using on-screen tools. The project will also greatly enhance children's geographical understandings, particularly in relation to the need to use standardised symbols on maps – not normally an aspect of geography covered at Key Stage 1. Inspection evidence suggests that ICT can have a transforming effect on children's geographical learning: Ofsted (2002) states that: 'Where ICT is used effectively to enhance pupils' geographical learning, it [results] in challenging work and high achievement.'

See *Maths* Project 4 (*Exploring with directions*), in which children work with LOGO software to control a screen turtle's movements around various maps, and *Arts* Project 3 (*Designing an environment*) for related activities.

References and further reading

Ofsted (Office for Standards in Education) (2002) *Ofsted Subject Reports. 2000/01: Primary Geography.* London: Ofsted.

HISTORY/SENSE OF TIME

Project Fact Card: Project 3: Using an information source

Who is it for?

- 5- to 7-year-olds (NC Levels 1–3)

What will the children do?

As part of a study of everyday life for men, women and, particularly, children during the Victorian period, pupils will search for specific information on a relevant website. They will enter a simple search term and choose an appropriate web page from a list of search results. They will carry out web-based activities and select key points or facts in answer to their questions.

What should the children know already?

- How to point and click with mouse and pointer to initiate actions on screen
- How to activate hyperlinks by pointing and clicking on text and/or icons
- How to enter simple text on screen using the keyboard

What do I need to know?

- The Uniform Resource Locator (URL) of an appropriate website for use as an information source, e.g. Virtual Victorians – www.victorians.org.uk
- Appropriate search terms for pupils to use to access information on the site

What resources will I need?

- A historical information source on the Web (such as Virtual Victorians – www.victorians.org.uk) or on a CD-ROM (such as *How We Used to Live: Early Victorians* or *How We Used to Live: Late Victorians* by Granada Learning)

What will the children learn?

- To search using simple search terms
- To select appropriate search results from a list
- To manipulate objects on screen in the context of a web-based activity or simulation

How to challenge the more able

- Use a more advanced information source with a more sophisticated search tool
- Copy and paste text into a simple word processor

How to support the less able

- Provide support from an adult to help in the search process
- Pre-select web pages containing appropriate information

Why teach this?

- The project is targeted on ICT NC KS1 PoS statements 1a, 1c and 2d.
- It also addresses History NC KS1 PoS statements 2b, 4a and 4b.
- The project augments and extends the content of QCA ICT Scheme of Work Units 1C and 2C.
- It provides appropriate ICT content for QCA History Scheme of Work Unit 1: *How are our toys different from those in the past?* and/or Unit 2: *What were homes like a long time ago?*

Using an information source

What will the children do?

As part of a study of home life in the Victorian period, children should make comparisons between the toys and everyday objects found in their homes and those that may have been found in a Victorian household. For young children, the ideal way to do this is through handling of artefacts, either genuine or reproduction, from the Victorian period. The comparisons can then be rooted in hands-on experience and direct comparison between comparable objects, e.g. a Victorian flat-iron and a modern 'iron'. Many museums have education services which will loan boxes of appropriate objects to schools, e.g. Warrington Museum (www.warrington.gov. uk/entertainment/museum/home.htm) offers boxes labelled 'Victorian Kitchen', 'Grandma's Kitchen', 'Tin Toys' and 'Traditional Wooden Toys'. As well as comparing objects, children can also be encouraged to identify household items for which there is no direct modern equivalent.

Although not intended as a replacement for first-hand experience, this project makes use of a 'virtual' loan box of objects from Tiverton Museum in Devon. The objects are represented electronically, on the Virtual Victorians website (www. victorians.org.uk), in the form of images, animations and VR (virtual reality) objects. Prior to the first activity, introduce children to some of the objects that might have been found in a middle-class home in the late nineteenth century. Either after handling objects or a discussion using pictures, make a list of items that the children would like to find out more about. Prompt to make sure that toys and objects featured in the site are included in the list.

Activity 1: Searching and search results

Using a large screen connected to a networked computer, show the home page of the Virtual Victorians website and explain that the site contains lots of information and activities about Victorian life. Show some sample pages, using the links on the left-hand side of the screen. Explain that, because the website has a large number of pages, it would take a long time to find out information about a specific household item or toy, by just browsing from page to page. Point out the 'Search box' on the home page and explain that, by entering a word into the box, it is possible to find specific pages of information very quickly. As an example, type the word 'doll' in the box and click the **Go** button. A page displaying the search results will appear very quickly. Explain that the page shows the results of the search, with ten links listed on the first page. The search tool will have listed the results in order of relevance with the most appropriate page, in relation to the search term, at the top – click the first link to go to a page about 'Florrie', a typical porcelain doll from the Victorian period. Show the children how to navigate back to the list of search results by clicking on the **Back** button on the toolbar.

After showing the children other pages listed in the search results (and making the point that pages further down the list will be less relevant to the search term), tell them that you want them to work in small groups and find out about other toys and objects from a Victorian house. Make the point that the items shown on the pages are all objects from relatively wealthy homes and poorer people would not have had so many possessions. Refer to the list made earlier and either assign objects to the groups or let the children decide for themselves what item from the list they would like to research. Tell the children that you want them to find out at least one fact about the item – focusing particularly on how it is different to a modern object. Explain that they can record their information in any way they like – by drawing on paper, making notes, or simply remembering – but they must be prepared to talk about their findings to the rest of the class in a plenary. Also explain that most of the items have on-screen activities linked to them and the children will have an opportunity to try some of these in a later session.

Get the children to work in their groups and monitor their searching closely – intervene, when necessary, to make the point about the most relevant results being at the top of the list on the 'Results page'. The session should be set within a relatively short time frame (to emphasise the point about the speed of web searching) and may be carried out by a whole class working on internet-linked computers in an ICT suite or by groups, on a rota basis, using an internet-linked classroom computer. Encourage the children to identify key facts about the objects and prompt them to record in appropriate ways.

At the end of the session, gather the children together for a plenary and get individuals from each group to report back on their object and what they have found out. To end the plenary, ask the children to compare the experience of using the website with any hands-on experience they have had with artefacts. Ask questions, such as: 'What did you find out from the website that you could not find out handling an object?' or 'Is looking at a picture of an object or reading some text about it better or not as good as handling a real object?'

Activity 2: On-screen activities

The second activity should be, to an extent, a repeat of the first, but with two differences: firstly, the groups should search for information on a different Victorian object; and, secondly, they should engage with the on-screen activities related to the objects that they find. Gather children together again so that all can see the website home page and enter a search term – 'bricks' is a good choice because the first link in the search results goes directly to an open-ended on-screen activity, involving the use of a 'virtual' set of wooden building blocks in a variety of shapes. Show the children how, by clicking and dragging, it is possible to build a simple structure using the bricks. When a structure has been created, show the children how to print the web page as a record of what they have done – you may decide to skip this step, if printing is in any way problematic on your computer or network.

Split the children into small groups and assign a search term to each group by means of cards with terms such as 'doll', 'bricks' or 'Fantascope' written on each one. Encourage children to take turns when engaged in activities and set the groups to work. When children are working on the activities, prompt them to think about ways in which the Victorian toys and objects are similar and different to modern equivalents.

At the end of the session, gather the children together for a plenary and get individuals from each group to report back on the activities that they have carried out. Focus your questions on comparisons between the Victorian toys and toys that children play with now. As several activities on the site enable users to make decisions and explore alternatives, encourage the children to describe the processes by which they produced their finished products, e.g. how they dressed the doll, how they built a structure using the building bricks, how they completed one of the jigsaw photographs. Get the children to recognise that ICT enabled them to make alterations and changes that would have been difficult or impossible by other means.

What should the children know already?

To complete the activities in this project, children will need to know how to point and click with a mouse to initiate actions on screen. If they have completed Project 1, the necessary skills for completion of the on-screen activities on the Virtual Victorians website should be in place. If they have not used web-based activities before, then they will need to be introduced to the concept of hyperlinks and will also need step-by-step guidance on how to drag and drop on-screen objects.

As the main focus of this project is the use of a search tool, the children will obviously need to know how to enter text using a keyboard. They will also need guidance on how to identify the on-screen field or 'Search box' in which search terms are entered. Moving the mouse pointer to this box and identifying when it becomes a blinking cursor (indicating readiness for text entry) are also skills which will need some direct tuition – adults using web search tools tend to take these skills for granted, but children can find precise movement of the mouse pointer quite tricky and become deeply frustrated when text that they have carefully typed using the keyboard does not appear on screen because the 'Search box' has not been clicked on properly.

What do I need to know?

The Uniform Resource Locator (URL) of an appropriate website for use as an information source

Before beginning this project, you will need to become familiar with the layout and content of an appropriate ICT information source for history at Key Stage 1. The Virtual Victorians website (www.victorians.org.uk) is a large and extensive site with material for the whole primary age-range and some content that could be used by older children and adults. Several factors make it particularly appropriate for the purposes of this project. Although some sections feature relatively large amounts of text-based information, which would be unsuitable for Key Stage 1 children, the descriptions of specific toys and objects are short, uncomplicated and enlivened by engaging images. The search tool on the site's home page is large, clear and simple – a large text-entry box with a **Go** button to its right. Once a search term has been entered, the search is quick and efficient. Although the search results are presented as a list of items, the descriptions are brief and the list is arranged effectively into an order of relevance to the search term. Clicking on the first item in the list will invariably go to the most relevant page.

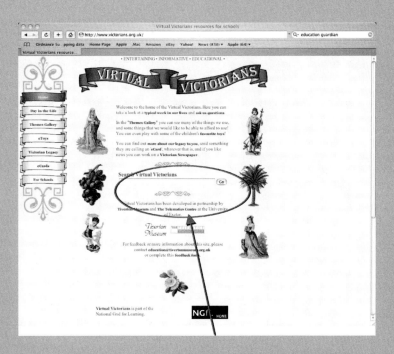

The Virtual Victorians home page with the search tool clearly indicated

Appropriate search terms for pupils to use to access information on the site

For Key Stage 1 children and the purposes of this project, you need to know which are the most appropriate sections of the site and, most importantly, which search terms will yield the best results in terms of factual information and on-screen tasks. The list below is not exhaustive, but gives a good indication of possibilities. The following search terms link to pages with text-based information and on-screen activities – some are suitable only for the guided search using cards suggested in Activity 2:

- ⊙ 'Doll' links to a page about 'Florrie', a typical Victorian porcelain doll, and an activity which enables children to dress her – Florrie's layers of clothes must be put on in the right order.

- ⊙ 'Bricks' goes to a page about wooden building blocks and an open-ended activity in which children can build a structure using drag and drop.

- ⊙ 'Decoupage' was the popular Victorian art of cutting out objects and arranging them on paper. Children can create their own 'virtual' decoupage, which can be printed out.

- ⊙ 'Lantern' links to information about a Victorian 'Magic Lantern' (an early form of slide projector) and there are some short slide shows to explore.

- ⊙ Fantascopes were one of the first forms of animation and 'Fantascope', as a search term, links to information about these revolving devices – children can view some typical animations, but care needs to be taken because the on-screen representations use strobe-like effects which may be unsuitable for some children.

- ⊙ 'Puzzle' links to pages containing late Victorian photographs which have been split into simple jigsaws or *ePuzzles* – although each picture can be assembled using drag and drop, children may find the activity quite difficult because the scenes are unfamiliar.

- ⊙ The terms 'Mysterion' and 'Kairosithon' go to quite challenging activities involving the interpretation of pictures of artefacts and sequencing of objects – although the ICT skills required are straightforward, the activities involve the application of quite advanced historical skills and processes.

Other search terms (e.g. 'Marbles', 'Rocking horse' and 'Rattle') go to pages of information and images – some with a rollover effect, activated by the mouse pointer, which switches between a picture of the toy or object and a picture showing it in context.

*The search results page of Virtual Victorians showing the
results of a search using the term 'rattle'*

The technical skills required by the project are relatively straightforward, e.g. the search tool does not require knowledge of Boolean search terms, such as AND, OR or NOT, and anyone who has carried out a search using a web search tool, such as Google or Lycos, will find it undemanding in terms of personal skills. One important technical point to note, however, is that the site requires *Microsoft Internet Explorer* to be used as your web browser. Other browsers, such as *Firefox* or *Safari*, can be used to carry out searches and to browse from page to page, but the on-screen activities only function in *Internet Explorer v.5* or later for Windows or Macintosh. Fortunately, all modern PCs or Macs will have the software pre-installed.

What will the children learn?

The project aims to introduce the basic principles of searching large databases of information using an ICT tool. Children will learn the skills of

⊙ identifying a 'Search box';

⊙ entering a search term or keyword using a keyboard;

⊙ activating a search by clicking on an on-screen button;

⊙ selecting an appropriate link from a page of search results.

The Key Ideas (from QCA ICT Scheme of Work Units 1C and 2C) that 'information comes from a variety of sources and can be presented in a variety of forms' and that 'appropriate search techniques [can be used to] find information' are covered within a meaningful and relevant subject context. The project also offers an opportunity to further develop children's understanding of the provisionality of ICT. As in Projects 1 and 2, ICT enables children to try things out and quickly make changes/alterations – not all of the on-screen activities encountered during Activity 2 have this potential, but several (notably 'Florrie the doll', the 'Building bricks' and 'Decoupage') provide good contexts for discussion, decision making and experimentation.

ICT enables the process of historical enquiry to be developed effectively in a Key Stage 1 context – children will quickly find answers to their questions and make comparisons between ways of life then and now, using accurate representations of 'real' sources. Although Virtual Victorians should ideally not be a replacement for hands-on experience of Victorian objects, it provides a rich resource offering elements of kinaesthetic experience, feedback and interaction, through the on-screen activities.

Challenging the more able and supporting the less able: modifying the project for older and younger pupils

Although more experienced learners could benefit from use of a more advanced information source, with a more sophisticated search tool, the Virtual Victorians website has tremendous potential, in itself, for further ICT-based challenges. For example, the eCards section of the site allows users to send an electronic postcard to an e-mail address – there is a range of Victorian images to choose from and a space on the 'card' for a short message. A more experienced user of the Web could send a fact, gleaned from one of the object-based pages, to a friend or a home e-mail address, thus sharing his/her historical knowledge with a wider audience. Alternatively, the site offers the facility for children to send a question to a 'Virtual Victorian' using a web-based form. The resource requires registration via e-mail, but is free. Members of a family living in the year 1874 answer questions sent – further information about the family is available on the extensive 'Day in the Life' section of the site. More fluent readers will find many further challenges on the site, e.g. a Victorian factory logbook or a Victorian newspaper to be deciphered.

In terms of ICT skills, the project offers scope for the more experienced to move on to skills involving the switching of applications. Instead of making handwritten notes, drawing pictures or remembering facts, more skilled learners could copy text on a web page and transfer it to a word processor using the **Paste** command. The text could then be edited and enhanced for printing or on-screen presentation. Virtual Victorians is, of course, not the only information source that could be used for the project. The 'How We Used to Live' series of CD-ROMs, published by Granada Learning, offers detailed information and a search facility by means of an index. Although intended for Key Stage 2, the CD-ROMs would be an appropriate information source for more able learners at Key Stage 1.

Less experienced learners will need support to complete the project. Although the images and animations on the Virtual Victorians site are accessible for non-readers, adult help will be needed during the search process. For the less able, it may be appropriate to bypass the search process, and provide access to suitable pages of information through pre-selected Bookmarks or Favorites. If you choose to do this, you will need to find appropriate pages and save them to the **Favorites** list in *Internet Explorer* using the **Add to Favorites . . .** command in the **Favorites** menu. The chosen pages can then be accessed from the list in the **Favorites** menu (see Project 5 for more information).

Why teach this?

The project augments and extends the content of QCA ICT Scheme of Work Units 1C: *The information around us* and 2C: *Finding information,* by providing an additional context for collecting information and carrying out straightforward lines of enquiry. It provides appropriate ICT content for QCA History Scheme of Work Unit 1: *How are our toys different from those in the past?* and/or Unit 2: *What were homes like a long time ago?,* if the chosen period of study is the late nineteenth century or 'Victorian' period.

As well as meeting key National Curriculum requirements at Key Stage 1 and addressing the techniques and Key Ideas from QCA Scheme of Work Units 1C and 2C in a meaningful historical context, the project is centred on a website which embodies much best practice in online learning using museum resources.

Research by Schaller *et al.* (2002) identified six different types of activity evident on museum websites – creative play, guided tour, interactive reference, puzzle/mystery, role play/stories and simulation. Of these, they found that puzzles and role-play activities seemed to have the greatest learning potential for young children. Describing them as 'Goal Based Scenarios' (GBS) with intrinsic rewards, Schaller *et al.* state that they offer 'a goal or challenge, a payoff, structure and guidance, and some degree of interactivity' (2002). On the Virtual Victorians site, several activities have the characteristics of a GBS, notably the 'Florrie the doll', 'Building bricks', 'Decoupage' and 'ePuzzles' activities. The elements of personal choice and play are likely to engage children's interest and lead to high-quality learning.

See *Arts* Project 2 (*Aboriginal art*) and *Science* Project 10 (*Using search engines*) for related activities.

References and further reading

Schaller, D. T. , Allison-Bunnell, S. and Chambers M. B. (2002) 'How do you like to learn? Comparing user preferences and visit length of educational web sites', in D. Bearman and J. Trant (eds), *Museums and the Web 2002: Selected Papers from an International Conference*. Pittsburgh, NJ: Archives & Museums Informatics. Available online at www.archimuse.com/mw2002/papers/schaller/schaller.html.

RELIGIOUS EDUCATION

Project Fact Card: Project 4: A virtual tour of a place of worship

Who is it for?

- 6- to 7-year-olds (NC Levels 1–3)

What will the children do?

Use hyperlinks to navigate around an on-screen representation of a place of worship. Make collaborative decisions about the duration, direction and content of a virtual tour. Compare the places of worship viewed on screen to real places.

What should the children know already?

- How to control effects on screen by pointing, dragging and clicking the mouse
- How to explore visual and text-based information using hyperlinks
- That a computer representation allows the user to make choices and that different decisions produce different outcomes

What do I need to know?

- The location (URLs) of websites which feature virtual tours of places of worship
- How to navigate around a chosen virtual tour
- How to navigate around a panoramic image, e.g. a *QuickTime* VR movie or *iPix* image
- The significant features of a chosen place of worship, including symbols

What resources will I need?

- A web browser, with the *QuickTime* plug-in installed

What will the children learn?

- To use hyperlinks to navigate around a visual information source
- To explore options and make choices in the context of a computer representation of a real place
- To gather information from a mainly visual information source
- To compare exploration of a computer representation of a place with first-hand experience

How to challenge the more able

- Use a more sophisticated virtual tour which includes linked panoramic images
- Use a virtual tour which connects information in a non-linear way through both visual and text-based hyperlinks
- Use a virtual tour of a more unfamiliar, unusual or unconventional place of worship

How to support the less able

- Use a simpler virtual tour where information is linked in a conventional, linear manner
- Use a place of worship which has obvious similarities to a place visited first hand by children
- Provide more structure and guidance to support information gathering, e.g. a short set of enquiry questions related to the place of worship

Why teach this?

- The activity is targeted on ICT NC KS1 PoS statements 1a and 2d.
- The activity augments and extends the content of QCA ICT Scheme of Work Units 2C and 2E.
- The activity supports teaching and learning about places of worship, which is a key element of the programme of study for KS1 in the QCA national framework for religious education and the QCA Religious Education Scheme of Work Unit 2D: *Visiting a place of worship – Generic.*

A virtual tour of a place of worship

What will the children do?

A virtual tour of a place of worship could be used as a replacement for an actual visit or to supplement first-hand experience. In the latter case, Activity 1 should follow on from a visit to a real place of worship in the locality. The virtual tour that the children explore should provide an extension and a contrast to the real place of worship – it may be a tour of a different place of worship from the same faith community or a tour of a place of worship of a different faith. The faith chosen, however, should be one that children have studied or will study in depth – it is important that the children, as virtual tourists, engage fully with the purpose of the visit and gain the most from it in educational terms.

A virtual tour could be used as a replacement for a real visit for several legitimate reasons. In some localities it may not be possible to arrange a visit to a place of worship of a particular faith, either because of distance or because the chosen faith community is small and a whole-class visit would be inconvenient and an imposition. If used as a replacement, it is important to raise with the children early on that the tour they will be experiencing will only give a restricted sense of place – with sights and possibly sounds, but no smells, tastes or textures to touch. If possible, during Activity 1, provide other sensory inputs to augment the on-screen experience – if the virtual tour has no sound, you could play some quiet music in the background and, perhaps, burn incense, if appropriate.

Activity 1: A virtual visit to a place of worship

For the first activity a large screen is essential – if accessing the virtual tour from a website on the internet, the computer used must be linked to the network. As a whole class, gather children together so that they can all see the screen. If possible, dim the lights so that children's attention is focused. Explain to the children that they are going to visit a place of worship using the computer. In this first activity, they will be visiting as a whole class, but later they will be working in small groups to find out about the place of worship independently. Explain that you are going to show them how to move around the tour and indicate some places that you want them to look at carefully later.

Before starting the tour, explain that although the place of worship they are visiting is made up of images on screen, to members of the faith it is still a very special place and the children need to follow certain rules and conventions when visiting, e.g. visitors to a mosque, a Hindu Mandir or a Sikh Gurdwara must remove their shoes and cover their heads before entering. Before proceeding, make sure that children carry out an applicable convention. Open the first web page and, using explanation, prompting and questioning, show the children how to navigate around the site. Pay particular attention to navigating panoramic images – ask children what sounds, smells, textures there might be in this place.

Tell children that you want them to look for symbols or special symbolic objects of the chosen religion in the place of worship – but not to shout out or put hands up when they see them, as that would not be appropriate. Show the class that they can explore the place of worship by different routes using the virtual tour. Also make the point that the tour on screen enables the viewer to see and to go to parts of the place of worship that would be inaccessible in reality, either because it is a very sacred part or would be unsafe. Finally, close the virtual tour and ask children about any symbols or objects that they saw. To end the activity, children put shoes back on or perform another action to indicate that they are leaving the place of worship.

Activity 2: Choosing a route and looking for symbols

This could follow on immediately from the first activity in some settings, e.g. an ICT suite, or be spread over several sessions if using a classroom computer. Ask children to navigate around the chosen virtual tour. Emphasise that they can choose their own route, but when working with partners, they must discuss and make a collective decision about which way to go. As they go through the tour, the children should note down (either using words or drawings) any special symbols or objects that they see and the names of any special parts of the place of worship. When viewing panoramic images, they should take it in turns to move the mouse pointer around and to use the in/out buttons to zoom in and out.

In a plenary, ask children to share the routes they used to explore the virtual tour, the symbols and objects that they spotted and any special words. Ask them how they think the tour was different to going to the real place. Explain the meaning (if applicable) of any symbols and objects that the children have spotted.

Activity 3: What is missing?

Remind children how to navigate around the chosen virtual tour and explain that, this time when exploring, you want them to think about what the virtual tour might be missing out. Tell them that you want them to record (either using words or drawings) the smells, textures, feelings and sounds (not applicable if the tour features a soundtrack) that they think they would sense in at least three places on the tour. Again stress that they can choose their own routes around the place of worship.

In a plenary, record a class list of smells, textures, feelings and sounds with contributions from all the groups. Ask children to talk to a partner about what they have learned about the place of worship and what they have learned about navigating around a virtual tour. Children report back one thing their partner has learned.

What should the children know already?

To engage with this project, pupils need to have developed skills of pointing, clicking and dragging with a mouse or other input device. They should understand that a computer representation allows the user to make choices and that different decisions produce different outcomes. The Y1 units in the QCA ICT Scheme of Work develop these skills. Children who have experienced Projects 1 and 3 in this book will also have the requisite skills.

What do I need to know?

The location (URLs) of websites which feature virtual tours of places of worship

The key technical skills that you will require for this project are similar to those for other web-based projects, e.g. typing a web address (URL) in a web browser, navigating web pages using hyperlinks and use of the **Back** button, where necessary, to return to a previously viewed page. You will need to know the location of some appropriate virtual tour websites (examples listed below) and be familiar with the conventions of your chosen tour.

How to navigate around a chosen virtual tour

If internet access is unreliable, you may wish to download your chosen virtual tour to your computer's hard disk or your local network server before starting Activity 1. This can be done quite easily using offline browsing software, which will download all the pages, images and other resources in a selected website. *WebStripper* for Windows is an example of such software – available for download from www.webstripper.net. Note, however, that some virtual tour sites (especially those with panoramic images) are very large and you will need to check that your hard disk or server has adequate free space to accommodate the site. A high-speed broadband connection is also highly desirable, as downloading even a relatively small site could take considerable time over a dial-up connection.

How to navigate around a panoramic image, e.g. a *QuickTime VR* movie or *iPix* image

Although panoramic images are not an absolutely essential component to include in this project, their potential for involving and immersing children in the tour (see 'Why teach this?', below) make them a particularly valuable element. VR (virtual reality) images are common on virtual tour websites and, regardless of the technology used to produce them, they all have the following characteristics and functions:

⊙ They provide a 360° panoramic view of a place – some also allow the viewer to look up and down.
⊙ The user can move the image around by moving the mouse pointer over the scene, usually with the left mouse button held down.
⊙ The image can be zoomed in and out using +/− buttons at the foot of the image viewer – often there are also keyboard shortcuts which perform the same functions: SHIFT (⇧) to zoom in, Control (Ctrl) to zoom out.

Depending on the format of the panoramic images in the chosen tour, you may need to install plug-in software into the web browser to view the images. *QuickTime VR* images require the installation of the *QuickTime* plug-in which can be downloaded and installed easily from the Apple Computer website – www.quicktime.com. Other formats use Java software that will probably already be installed on your computer, whether Windows PC or Macintosh. As with all projects, a certain amount of preparation will be needed before the first lesson. Do not assume that you will be able to view images on the sites listed below without checking first.

The significant features of a chosen place of worship, including symbols

The subject knowledge about a particular faith required for a chosen virtual tour will depend, of course, on the place of worship. The symbols and words children will encounter will be very different for a synagogue, a Christian church or a mosque. You will need to familiarise yourself with the meanings of symbols, such as the star of David and the cross or Ganesh. You will also need to be confident about the purpose and meanings of different parts of a chosen place of worship, e.g. the Minaret, the Mihrab and the Minbar in a mosque.

Examples of virtual tours of places of worship

This is an indicative, not exhaustive list; a fuller list of available sites can be found at www.placesofworship.org.uk

⊙ **Hanley Synagogue** – www.spirit-staffs.co.uk/synagogue/index1.htm
Although the images in this site are not panoramic, it offers some choice in terms of navigation and makes use of short video clips to explain symbols and functions of parts of the synagogue.
⊙ **Cordoba Mosque** – www.panoramas.dk/fullscreen/fullscreen44.html
Two linked full-screen *QuickTime VR* panoramas showing the interior of a Moorish mosque in Spain.
⊙ **Guildford Cathedral** – www.surreyplacesofworship.org.uk/virtualvisits/cathedral/ks1.htm

⊙ **Portsmouth Cathedral** – www.portsmouthcathedral.org.uk/3dtour.htm

⊙ **York Minster** – http://www.vryork.com/minster/minster_index.html

⊙ **St Paul's Cathedral, London** – www.explore-stpauls.net

Tours containing linked panoramic images – the tour of St Paul's being the most sophisticated.

The Explore St Paul's Cathedral virtual tour
© 2003 Armchair Travel Co. Ltd.

⊙ **St Mary's Roman Catholic Church, Grimsby** – http://tlfe.org.uk/re/stmarys.htm

A tour of a parish church using hyperlinked images and simple text.

⊙ **The Sikhism Home Page** – www.sikhs.org/golden

A tour, using small panoramic images, of the Golden Temple of Amritsar in India.

⊙ **Amaravati Buddhist Monastery, Great Gaddesden, near Hemel Hempstead** – www.thegrid.org.uk/learning/re/virtual/buddhisttrail/index.shtml

A simple tour using mainly images.

What will the children learn?

This project will provide an introduction to the different forms that hyperlinks can take on web pages and elsewhere. All virtual tours use text-based links and several of those listed above also contain hyperlinked images and links within images (usually indicated by the mouse pointer taking the form of a pointing hand over part of the image). It will, therefore, provide a good grounding for children's independent research using web pages in subject contexts. The project develops key skills of visual literacy in that it encourages children to look closely at images and take in details. It also encourages them to consider the overall impression of an image and what might be missing in terms of other sensory experiences. This objective is not addressed specifically in any unit of the QCA ICT scheme.

The project encourages children to compare an on-screen representation with the real world as required by the 'Reviewing, modifying and evaluating work as it progresses' strand of the ICT National Curriculum. The project aims, through the third activity, to get children to articulate what might be missing from a virtual tour. During the activities it is also important to encourage them to think about the advantages of a virtual tour: routes can be changed easily, parts of a place of worship can be quickly revisited, a small faith community is not inconvenienced.

Challenging the more able and supporting the less able: modifying the project for older and younger pupils

The project could be modified in a number of ways to provide extra challenge or to meet the needs of older pupils. Children with more experience and greater confidence in the use of images and hyperlinks could be challenged by the use of a more sophisticated virtual tour, which includes linked panoramic images – the tour of St Paul's Cathedral is a good example. Although all the tours listed above offer choice in their navigation, some have a more challenging non-linear structure with different types of embedded hyperlinks and activities – the tour of an Antiochan Orthodox church (visit www.antiochian-orthodox.co.uk) uses images, text and detailed plans. The use of a virtual tour of a more unfamiliar, unusual or unconventional place of worship would also provide additional challenge. In the listing above, the tours of the Cordoba mosque and the Golden Temple at Amritsar have an added element of unfamiliarity because of their location in distant places and different cultures.

For the less confident users of ICT and younger pupils, a simpler virtual tour could be used. The tour of St Mary's Roman Catholic Church in Grimsby is a good example of a tour where information is linked in a generally conventional, linear manner. Younger children would also benefit from being presented with a place of worship which has similarities to a place visited at first hand – if children have visited a local Christian church, then a virtual tour of a Christian cathedral would enable them to identify familiar features, while still appreciating a contrast in size and scale. Finally, younger children's information gathering could be supported by a more structured set of questions or a writing frame linked closely to the chosen tour.

Why teach this?

The project augments and extends the content of QCA ICT Scheme of Work Units 2C: *Finding information* and 2E: *Questions and answers* by giving experience of visual, web-based information sources. It also aims to develop skills of visual literacy, which are largely ignored by the scheme. The project makes appropriate use of visual, web-based sources to support teaching and learning about places of worship. Visits to such places are a key element of the programme of study for KS1 in the QCA national framework for religious education and the QCA religious education scheme of work. In Y2, Unit 2D of the scheme focuses on the structure of a generic visit to a place of worship. The QCA national framework also requires that Key Stage 1 children gain experience of Christianity and another religious community.

This project contributes significantly to the development of essential cross-curricular skills, in particular the skills of visual literacy. Research evidence (Aldrich and Sheppard 2000; Pickford 2004) suggests that children in this age-range need to be taught the skill of 'reading' visual images. The project sets out to give a context for teaching these skills – looking for details, taking in an overall impression of an image and also considering what the image does not show.

Pickford (2004: 117) suggests that panoramic images on screen may be particularly useful for developing these skills, as they lead to 'more sustained information gathering and some evidence of higher-order thinking in the form of interpretations and evaluative comments'. Although panoramas are not virtual reality applications in the fullest sense – quasi VR is one way of describing them – they do offer, educationally, some of the benefits of virtual reality applications: they have the potential to actualise learning 'by making an image more real than a two-dimensional picture' (Cronin 1997) and can provide a focus for collaboration leading to high quality learning.

See *Learning ICT in English* Project 7 (*Photo-dramas*) for related activities.

References and further reading

Aldrich, F. and Sheppard, L. (2000) '"Graphicacy": the fourth "R"?' *Primary Science Review*, 64, 8–11.

Cronin, P. (1997) 'Report on the applications of virtual reality technology to education'. Virtual Reality and Education Laboratory (VREL), College of Education, East Carolina University. Accessed May 2004 (http://citeseer.ist.psu.edu/context/1223087/0).

Pickford, T. (2004) 'What does this picture show?', in R. Bowles (ed.) *Register of Research in Primary Geography: Place and Space*. London: Register of Research.

GEOGRAPHY

Project Fact Card: Project 5: Repurposing information for different audiences

Who is it for?

- 7- to 9-year-olds (NC Levels 2–4)

What will the children do?

Select textual and graphical information from a book-marked list of web pages and carry out a search using a child-friendly search tool. Selected information will be used to create a desktop published document about a locality aimed at a specific audience, e.g. younger children, parents

What should the children know already?

- How to use hyperlinks to open web pages
- How to carry out a simple search using a search tool on CD-ROM or the Web
- How to copy and paste text and graphics within a document
- Writing for different audiences

What do I need to know?

- The location (URLs) of appropriate websites for the chosen context/topic
- How to add, organise and import/export bookmarks (Favorites) in a web browser
- The URL of a child-friendly web search tool, e.g. BBCi, and some simple search strategies
- How to copy information in text/graphic form from a web browser to a simple desktop publishing (DTP) program
- Basic functions of a chosen DTP program

What resources will I need?

- A web browser and a simple (DTP program), e.g. *Microsoft Publisher* or BlackCat *Writer 2.*

What will the children learn?

- To select appropriate information from a web-based source
- To copy and paste information in text/graphic form from one application (a web browser) to another (a DTP program)
- To arrange and rearrange text/graphic objects on a DTP page to make them appropriate for a target audience

How to challenge the more able

- Provide a more varied list of bookmarks
- Provide starting point questions which will require more advanced search strategies, e.g. using the Boolean operator: OR
- Provide a more demanding audience for the DTP document, e.g. someone whose first language is not English
- Use a more advanced DTP program which requires a greater understanding of layout options

How to support the less able

- Provide highly structured questions linked to specific websites
- Create a document containing appropriate text and graphics for pupils to edit and modify
- Use younger children as a target audience

Why teach this?

- The project is targeted on ICT NC KS2 PoS statements 1b, 2a and 3b.
- The project augments and extends the content of QCA ICT Scheme of Work Unit 4A and also fills a gap in the progression of the units between Y2 and Y5.
- The project makes appropriate use of web-based sources to support teaching and learning about contrasting localities as required by the Geography National Curriculum and the QCA Scheme of Work for Geography Units 10 and 13.

Repurposing information for different audiences

What will the children do?

After an initial introduction to the selected locality – Where is it? How far away? How could you get there? – pupils should go into co-operative groups to generate questions about the place. They should produce a set of questions agreed within the group and, after discussion with the teacher, create their own structured sheet of questions ready for the first activity.

Activity 1: Research using bookmarks

Working in small groups – mixed ability in terms of ICT and reading skills – get the pupils to open a prepared bookmark list of web pages about the chosen locality. The links should give a clear indication of the content of the linked web pages and some answers to basic questions about the place should be quickly found. Answers should be recorded on the structured question sheets. In a plenary at the end of the activity, identify questions that require further research. Ideally, the questions should relate to an issue which is important in the locality (and about which there are differing views), e.g. deforestation in a rainforest locality, a land-use conflict in a UK locality.

Activity 2: Copying and pasting between programs

Again working in small groups, pupils should use the BBCi website to carry out further research about the place (and the issue identified in Activity 1, if relevant). This time a word processor or desktop publishing (DTP) program should be running at the same time as the web browser.

When they find suitable text on a web page, pupils should highlight it and select **Copy** in the web browser's toolbar. The word processor/DTP program window should then be opened and the **Paste** command used to put the text into the word processor/DTP document. When an appropriate picture is found, get the pupils to right click on the image and select **Copy** from the resulting contextual menu. In the word processor/DTP program, select **Paste** to insert the image into the document.

When enough text and images have been found to answer the questions or to represent the differing views about an issue, the word processor/DTP document should be saved to disk.

Activity 3: Communicating to an audience

At the beginning of the third activity, pupils should be introduced to the possible audiences for their paper document, e.g. peers, younger pupils or parents. After some discussion of the needs/interests of the audience, pupils should open the saved document from Activity 2 and modify the content, layout and appearance according to their audience's demands/needs. Discussion in the working groups should focus on identifying the main points of the content and identifying a layout with maximum impact and clarity. At the end of the activity, the documents should be printed.

During a plenary session, pupils should display their finished documents and describe the reasons for their chosen layout and ways in which layouts could be developed and improved. They should compare the process they have been through to the use of 'traditional' means of research and presentation, e.g. use of books, newspapers, handwritten reports, cutting and pasting paper.

What should the children know already?

Prior to carrying out the first activity, pupils need to be familiar with the idea of hyperlinks and how to open a web page by clicking on hyperlinked text – covered in Project 3 in this book. If following the QCA ICT Scheme of Work, pupils will have encountered this Key Idea in Year 2 Unit 2C: *Finding information.* Combining text and graphics in a document and altering text in various ways is part of Unit 3A: *Combining text and graphics* in the scheme. The content of this project replaces and extends the content of Unit 4A: *Writing for different audiences*, which applies principles covered in Literacy to writing using ICT tools. The idea of factual writing for different audiences is covered extensively in literacy lessons by Y3/4.

What do I need to know?

The location (URLs) of appropriate websites for the chosen context/topic

The demands on a teacher's subject knowledge are relatively straightforward in that they relate to the use of everyday ICT tools. In terms of the geography content, you will need to have identified a number of websites that will provide answers to children's basic questions about the chosen locality (e.g. Where is it? What do people do there? What are homes like?) prior to beginning the project. Although the QCA

Geography Scheme of Work is not prescriptive about the localities that must be taught, many schools have chosen to focus on the localities identified by the scheme.

For Unit 10: *A village in India* (which links to the Chembakolli pack produced by Action Aid), possible starting points include:

- ⊙ www.chembakolli.com – Action Aid website with resources about the village (requires subscription)
- ⊙ www.nilgiris.tn.gov.in – website of the Nilgiris district of the State of Tamil Nadu, including a range of maps and images
- ⊙ www.mapsofindia.com/maps/tamilnadu/chembakolli.htm – maps at varying scales showing the location of the village
- ⊙ www.wunderground.com/global/stations/43317.html – detailed five-day weather forecast for the nearest large town
- ⊙ www.tamilglobe.com – website presenting Indian and world news from a South Indian perspective

For Unit 13: *A contrasting UK locality – Llandudno*, possible starting points include:

- ⊙ www.aboutbritain.com/towns/Llandudno.asp – general information page about Llandudno
- ⊙ www.llandudno-tourism.co.uk – tourist information website
- ⊙ www.llandudno.com – commercial website containing information and many images
- ⊙ www.llandudno-tourism.co.uk/asp/streetll.htm – street map
- ⊙ www.santsior.conwy.sch.uk – website of a local primary school
- ⊙ www.freefoto.com/browse.jsp?id=1059-02-0 – images of Llandudno

How to add, organise and import/export bookmarks (Favorites) in a web browser

Having identified appropriate links, you will then need technical knowledge relating to bookmarking and the creation of a web links page in your web browser. The following describes this process when using *Internet Explorer*.

Bookmarking

1. Once you have selected your locality, open *Internet Explorer* and select **Organize Favorites . . .** from the **Favorites** menu.
2. In the resulting dialogue, click the **Create Folder** button and type a name for your new folder.

   Click the **Close** button and begin your search. You may choose Google or another popular search tool to find your web links. If you want to be sure that the web pages that you find are appropriate for pupils, you may wish to use a child-friendly search tool. Some appropriate tools are:

   - ⊙ *Yahooligans* – www.yahooligans.com
   - ⊙ *KidsClick!* – http://sunsite.berkeley.edu/kidsclick!/
   - ⊙ *Ask Jeeves for Kids* – www.ajkids.com
   - ⊙ *BBCi* – www.bbc.co.uk/search (this has the advantage of being a UK-based site)

3. When you find an appropriate web page for inclusion in your web links list, select **Add to Favorites . . .** from the **Favorites** menu.

4. In the resulting dialogue:

- ⊙ give your link an appropriate title, if applicable
- ⊙ click on the **Create in** >> button and select the folder you created in Step 2
- ⊙ click on the **OK** button

5. Continue searching until you have found around a dozen relevant links about your locality. Repeat the steps in Step 5 for each link that you find.

Making a web links page

To turn your links into a web page that can be viewed in *Internet Explorer* or any other web browser, you need to export your Favorites as an HTML file. To do this:

1. Select **Import and Export . . .** from the **File** menu.
2. In the resulting dialogue (the Import/Export Wizard), click on **Next**.
3. In the next window, highlight **Export Favorites** from the list of options and click **Next**.

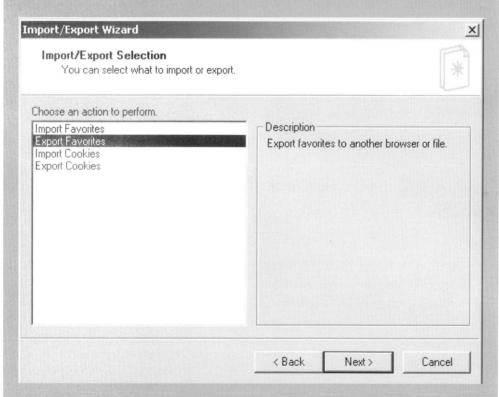

The Import/Export Selection *screen, in the Import/Export Wizard, with* Export Favorites *highlighted*

4. Click on the folder (created in Step 2 on the previous page) in the window and click **Next**.
5. In the next window, select the **Export to File or Address** option and click on the **Browse . . .** button.
6. Select a folder in which your web links page will be created – it could be the desktop or a network drive, for example.

7. In the next window, click on **Finish** and your web links page will be saved in the folder you selected.

8. When the **Successfully Exported Favorites** dialogue appears, click **OK** and either close or minimise the *Internet Explorer* window.

9. Open the folder in which you saved your web links page and you should see a file named 'bookmark.htm'. Double click on this file and your list of links should appear in an *Internet Explorer* window.

10. Click on the links to test your page. The page can now be saved to disk and loaded onto any networked computer ready for pupils to use for their research.

The URL of a child-friendly web search tool, e.g. BBCi, and some simple search strategies

Although there are several child-friendly search tools available on the Web, most are US in origin and rather US-centric in outlook. The BBCi website is UK based and is underpinned by Google technology. It is intended to be 'family friendly', using 'a combination of technology and regular human checks to detect and block offensive websites' (BBCi – www.bbc.co.uk/search/whysearch.shtml). Its disadvantage is that the main search engine does not support the standard Boolean search terms (AND, OR, NOT), but favours quotation marks (" ") and mathematical symbols ($+$, $-$) to search for exact phrases, words that must be included and words that must not be included in search results. BBCi's search results are usefully grouped into results from the Web, from BBC News and from the BBC site as a whole.

How to copy information in text/graphic form from a web browser to a simple desktop publishing (DTP) program

The main ICT skill that you will have to teach during this project is how to copy and paste text and images from one application (a web browser) to another (a word processor/DTP program). This is a relatively straightforward task requiring the two applications (programs) to be open simultaneously – a facility that is well within the capabilities of modern computers. The precise details of how to do this task with specific software may require you to consult the manual of your chosen word processor/ DTP software.

Once they are running, switching between applications on different computer platforms is achieved in the following ways:

⊙ On Windows 98/2000/ME/XP: Click on the button of the chosen program in the Taskbar at the foot of the screen – this will bring the program window to the front.

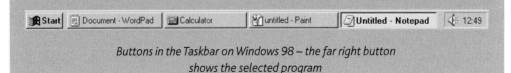

Buttons in the Taskbar on Windows 98 – the far right button
shows the selected program

⊙ On Macintosh OS X: Click on the required program's icon in the Dock at the foot of the screen or type 'Command-Tab' to bring up a window from which the program can be selected.

The Dock in Mac OS X – the second icon on the left shows the running program

Basic functions of a chosen DTP program

Finally, you will need to be familiar with the functions of your chosen word processor/ DTP program so that you can confidently support your pupils in the editing of their documents. For this project, a DTP program is preferable to a word processor because it is likely to give greater flexibility in laying out images and blocks of text on a page. What are the differences between the two types of programs?

Word processor:
A program used to create and print (chiefly textual) documents that might otherwise be prepared on a typewriter. The key advantage of [a] word processor is its ability to make changes easily, such as correcting spelling, changing margins, or adding, deleting, and relocating entire blocks of text. Once created, the document can be printed quickly and accurately and saved for later modifications.

Desktop publishing (DTP):
Using computers to lay out text and graphics for printing in magazines, newsletters, brochures etc. A good DTP system provides precise control over templates, styles, fonts, sizes, colour, paragraph formatting, images and fitting text into irregular shapes.

(FOLDOC [Free On-line Dictionary of Computing] 2004
– http://wombat.doc.ic.ac.uk/foldoc)

As can be seen from these definitions, essentially the differences between these two types of programs have become blurred over time – software, such as *Microsoft Word* (which began as a word processor), can provide a page view in which images and text blocks can be moved around and resized just like in a DTP program. From a primary school perspective, however, you will need to consider which software makes page layout easier and more straightforward for pupils. Using *Word*, pupils will need skills in the use of the **Drawing** and **Picture** toolbars and the commands in the **View** menu. More DTP-like primary software, such as *Textease* or *Granada Writer*, have far less confusing interfaces, with single toolbars containing all necessary commands for text and image manipulation. For older pupils, *Microsoft Publisher* is an effective choice – its opening view is full page and the main toolbar gives quick access to the main DTP functions.

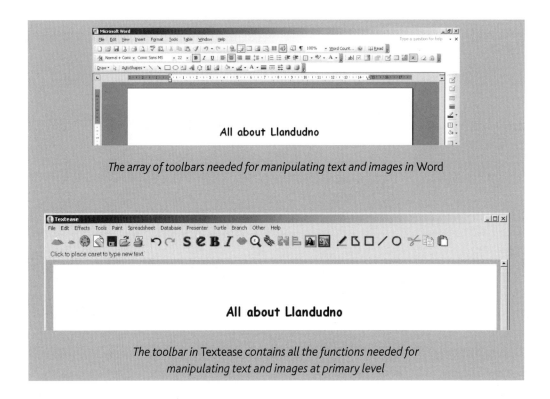

The array of toolbars needed for manipulating text and images in Word

The toolbar in Textease *contains all the functions needed for manipulating text and images at primary level*

What will the children learn?

Although pupils will have selected information before from the Web or CD-ROM (in ICT Scheme of Work Unit 2C, for example), this project will extend their skills by (a) setting the task within a clear geographical context, (b) giving scope for more sophisticated searching methods and (c) providing answers to questions they have generated themselves.

Different web search tools give scope for the development of different skills. If BBCi is used, pupils will gain experience of using quotation marks and +/− to search for exact phrases and to include and exclude from searches. Use of another web search tool (e.g. AltaVista – www.altavista.co.uk) may give access to the use of Boolean operators – AND/NOT to include/exclude from a search – but close supervision will be required to ensure that pupils do not access inappropriate websites. Most school networks have screening software installed to make sure that unsuitable sites are blocked, but practical experience suggests that these are by no means foolproof.

During Activity 3, observation of pupils will be required to ascertain the extent to which page layouts have been modified with audiences in mind. It may be useful to instruct pupils to print out their developing designs at regular intervals (say, every 10 minutes during a 30-minute activity) so that there is a paper record of the development of their finished product.

Challenging the more able and supporting the less able: modifying the project for older and younger pupils

The project could be modified in a number of ways to provide extra challenge or to meet the needs of older pupils. In Activity 1, a wider selection of web links could be provided, requiring pupils to select those that are appropriate and reject others as being irrelevant. In Activity 2, a full range of search strategies could be required to answer specific questions, e.g. a question about canals in Manchester, excluding the Ship Canal, would require the following to be typed into the BBCi search tool: 'canal + Manchester − ship' (other search tools would require: 'canal AND Manchester NOT ship'). In Activity 3, a more demanding audience could be selected for the document (e.g. people whose first language is not English, people who live in the locality concerned) and a more sophisticated DTP program could be used – *Microsoft Publisher* provides layout options, such as linked text boxes, not found in simpler primary school DTP tools.

For the less confident users of ICT and younger pupils, Activity 1 could be structured quite rigidly with the web links page providing single links leading to answers to specific questions. For example, the question 'Where is Llandudno?' could be followed by a link going straight to text, such as 'Llandudno is in the county of Conwy. It is a sweeping bay with a headland at each end of the bay' (Unofficial Guide to Llandudno 2003 – www.llandudno.cwc.net). In Activity 2, a website which supports natural language questions, such as 'Where is India?' could be used – *Ask Jeeves for Kids* (www.ajkids. com) being one example. For Activity 3, there are several ways in which the task could be supported: a younger target audience could be selected, a simple highly structured DTP program could be used (*2publish* by 2Simple Software, for example) or a document requiring fairly minimal editing could be provided.

Why teach this?

The project provides an excellent opportunity to discuss the strengths and weaknesses of the use of ICT for information gathering as required by the 'Reviewing, modifying and evaluating work as it progresses' strand of the ICT PoS. It augments and extends the content of QCA ICT Scheme of Work Unit 4A: *Writing for different audiences*, and also fills a gap in the progression of the units – between Y2 and Y5 there are no units which focus on web searching and the use of information gathered in this way in word-processed or DTP documents.

The project makes appropriate use of web-based sources to support teaching and learning about contrasting localities as required by the Geography National Curriculum and the QCA Scheme of Work for geography. In Y3/4, Units 10 and 13 of the scheme (relating to India and a contrasting UK locality: Llandudno) are particularly suitable contexts for web-based research and presentation of findings to different audiences.

The project contributes significantly to the development of essential cross-curricular skills. With the plethora of websites available for research across the curriculum, it is vital that pupils become critical users and interpreters of web-based information. The project aims to foster these critical skills through the use of the Web to answer targeted questions, at first, followed by more open searching for specific information. The project makes the needs of the audience the uppermost concern when repurposing information, thus fostering a critical approach to text and images found on the Web – Will this text make sense to younger children? Will parents understand this image or is a caption needed?

The structure of the project is obviously applicable across several curriculum areas in Key Stage 2. It could be used as a framework for finding and repurposing information in the contexts of history, art or religious education, for example. It is not intended as a rigid model, but the generation of questions by pupils, developing search strategies based on the questions and repurposing the information with an audience in mind, are necessary components, whatever the context.

Finally, it is worth noting that much of the text and many of the images found on the Web will be subject to copyright. You may be concerned that your pupils will be infringing copyright law by copying web content. Certainly, it would be unadvisable to distribute pupils' products beyond the school or charge for them, for example, as part of a school newspaper. The ins and outs of copyright law are far too complex for a detailed outline here – for a reasonably clear and lucid account of what can and cannot be done using web content, consult the Department for Education and Skills (DfES) Internet Safety website, specifically http://safety.ngfl.gov.uk/schools/document.php3?D=d69. Further copyright restrictions and exceptions are explained in Project 9 in this book.

See *Learning ICT in Science* Project 7 (*Multimedia information source*) and *English* Project 9 (*Creating an information website*) for related activities.

HISTORY

Project Fact Card: Project 6: Using a database to analyse census data

Who is it for?

- 7- to 10-year-olds (NC Levels 2–5)

What do I need to know?

- Where and how to obtain census data for the school's locality
- How to set up a database file

What will the children do?

Pupils will use database software and census data to find out about a household during the Victorian period, in the context of role play. They will find answers to questions about the locality during the Victorian period.

What should the children know already?

- How to search for information using simple search techniques, e.g. entering a search term into a web-based search tool

What resources will I need?

- A flat file database program, e.g. *Information Workshop 2000*

What will the children learn?

- How to search a database, looking for specific information, using more advanced searching techniques
- How to use the tools of a database package to answer questions

How to challenge the more able

- Pupils can set up a database file from scratch, by entering information from census records or by creating a census of the class
- Find answers to questions, using more sophisticated searching techniques and database tools

How to support the less able

- Use a simpler database package
- Provide more adult or peer support

Why teach this?

- The project is targeted on ICT NC KS2 PoS statements 1a, 1b and 1c.
- It supports and augments the content of QCA ICT Scheme of Work Units 4D, 5B and 5C.
- The project supports teaching and learning about historical enquiry (History National Curriculum KS2 PoS 4a, 4b) in the context of the study of Victorian Britain. In Y5/6, Units 11 and 12 of the QCA history scheme of work focus on Victorian Britain.

Using a database to analyse census data

What will the children do?

Although the relevant QCA primary history scheme of work units are located at Y5/6, the study of Victorian Britain, as a vehicle for the development of historical enquiry skills, can take place at any point in Key Stage 2, depending on the school's key stage plans. This project, therefore, is aimed at mid-KS2 and is easily adaptable to the needs of older or younger pupils. Victorian Britain is a particularly productive context for the development of enquiry skills because of the plethora of accessible primary source materials that are available, relating to the period. Local record offices and archives usually hold a huge number of sources from the period: from early OS maps to local photographs; from newspapers to school log books. A key resource, which most record offices and archives will have access to, are census records from the local area – if not for the whole Victorian period, then certainly for key years.

A general census has been conducted in this country every ten years since 1801. The first gathered only population figures for villages or towns. Since 1851, however, details of the members of each household have been collected and recorded in enumerators' schedules. The most recent available census is for 1901 – available online at www.1901census.nationalarchives.gov.uk. Prior to carrying out the Activity 1, you need to have gained access to census returns for a year in the late Victorian period, preferably for the school's locality, and entered information on some residents into a database program (prepared datafiles for areas of Chester and Warrington in Cheshire, for 1881 and 1901 respectively, are available on the CD). To make the activity worthwhile, your datafile should contain information on around 50 people with details, drawn from the census records, on each person. The activity will make most sense to children if the file contains information on people living in a defined geographical area that they know, e.g. a local street or a village. Prior to beginning the activity, you need to have explained what the census set out to do in the Victorian period. You also should have shown a sample census record to the children (it will be a photocopy of an original enumerator's schedule) so that they appreciate that the original documents, on which the activity is based, were handwritten on paper. Explain that the census gives information on real people under specific headings, e.g. name, age, occupation, etc. The ideal database software for the ICT activities is *Information Workshop* (available for Windows PC only, from BlackCat software – www.blackcatsoftware.com), although any Key Stage 2 database software should have the necessary capabilities.

Activity 1: Finding census information using database software

Gather children around a large screen. Explain that you have entered information, drawn from the census, into a database program. Ask the children why they think this might help in gathering information from the census. Make the point that ICT can speed up the process of information gathering (and make it easier) by carrying out a simple activity comparing the census in its two different forms. Give out a pile of photocopies of enumerators' schedules to a group of children. Ask them to find a specific person on the census, within a time limit. The children will not only have to cope with shuffling through several sheets of paper, but they will also have to decipher the Victorian handwriting. If the children succeed in finding the person, get them to read out the information available on the person and the others in their household.

Now show the children how much more quickly and easily we can find out the same information using ICT. Start *Information Workshop* and show the layout of the database file – make the point that the file contains the same information as the enumerators' schedules, but is simpler and easier to read because it has been transcribed. Demonstrate a search for the same person as before. In *Information Workshop*, access the search functions by clicking the 'Search' icon in the toolbar – it is represented by a symbol showing two eyes. Enter the name as a search term, confirm and click on the 'Search' button. When the software finds the name almost instantly, contrast this with the amount of time taken to search through the paper records.

Next, show how to find the others in the household. Get the children to make a note of the person's address. Make sure that all the records are selected again (in *Information Workshop*, select **All Records** from the **View** menu) and start a new search. This time enter the address of the person. Make the point that Victorian households often contained more than one family, so searching for a family name might not show everyone who lived in a household – poorer households could be made up of several families and middle-class families often had servants. Enter the address as a search term, confirm, and click on the 'Search' button. Again, make the point about the speed of the search. The records for all the people living at the address will be displayed.

If children are unfamiliar with databases and their structure, the second part of Activity 1 should consist of some hands-on experience with the software. Provide the children with cards printed with the names of people in the datafile and get the children to work, in small groups, on finding the relevant records using the simple search functions you have demonstrated. If children are more experienced, you could move directly on to Activity 2.

Activity 2: A visit by the census enumerator

Set up the scenario for Activity 2 in the following way. Explain that, at tremendous expense, you have built a time machine in school and soon you are going to switch it on! After a short period of warming up, the time machine is going to go back to the year of your chosen census, say 1881, and bring back the census enumerator to do a final check on the census. When the enumerator steps out of the time machine, he will think that he is still in 1881 (enumerators were nearly always male) and that the children in the class are the residents of the street or village that he is responsible for. He will go through his copy of the census and ask questions of the children – it is very important that they are able to answer them, so the enumerator does not suspect he has come forward in time!

Tell the children that they are going to 'become' the residents of the street or village for the enumerator's visit. Distribute cards with names of the people in the census – preferably one for each pupil, but children could work in small groups if they are inexperienced. Within a short time frame, they need to find out the following information about the person whose name is on the card:

⊙ Address

⊙ Relationship in the household – head, wife, son, daughter, lodger?

⊙ Married or unmarried?

⊙ Age

⊙ Occupation – are you an employer or an employee?

⊙ Where were you born?

⊙ How many brothers or sisters?

⊙ How many children? their names? their ages?

Tell the pupils that they need to be prepared for any unexpected questions! The census enumerator has a reputation for checking thoroughly that all information is correct and no-one is trying to evade the census. The children may need to use their imaginations to 'make up' answers to unexpected questions, based on the available evidence and their background knowledge about the Victorians. They also need to check up on who lives next door and over the road so that you can answer any questions about neighbours.

Set the children to work, emphasising that they have little time, so must take advantage of the speed of the database software. Organisation of the activity will depend greatly on resources and time available. You could do the activity in one session in an ICT suite or computer room. Or you could run the activity over a longer period, using a classroom computer accessed on a rota basis. You might want to make the enumerator's visit the conclusion of a topic on the Victorians, with children dressing up in appropriate clothes and even decorating the classroom, so the enumerator feels at home.

However it is organised, give children appropriate support during the search for information – emphasise the importance of entering names accurately and noting down key facts in preparation for the enumerator's questions. Encourage children to help each other in the search. When time is up for the search, you may want to 'announce' the enumerator's arrival with a suitable time machine sound effect.

The enumerator could be an adult that the children do not know or you could take on the role yourself – dressing up in, at least, a Victorian top hat is a good idea. Whoever takes on the role, the enumerator should ask his questions with some authority. Some questions should be straightforward checks on names and ages. Others should ask for numbers in households and information on neighbours. The enumerator could also make some erroneous statements that the children have to, politely, correct. To conclude the activity, the enumerator might go back to his time machine, taking a Victorian artefact that the children have made or, simply, announce the end of the role play in an appropriate manner – the Victorians loved grandiose, flowery language.

In a plenary, out of role, discuss with the children the benefits of using ICT for the activity. Get them to discuss the search and how they felt when answering the enumerator's questions. Some children can take the role play very seriously and need a detailed debriefing.

Activity 3: Using the census to answer enquiry questions

The third and final activity should focus on questions that can be answered about the locality during the Victorian period. Gather children together so that they can see the computer screen and explain that use of the database enables us to quickly find answers to more general questions, as well as specific information about individuals. Suggest some possible questions and encourage children to come up with others – possible questions could include: 'What was the most common occupation in our area in 1881?'; 'Were most of the people in the census born in our locality or did they come from elsewhere?'; 'At what age did children leave school in 1881?'; or 'What was the largest household in 1881?' Make a list of possible questions on a large sheet of paper or a board. Select one from the list that could be answered using a more complex search, for example 'How many servants were under 16?'

Show the children how to find an answer to the question using a more advanced search.

1. If using *Information Workshop*, click on the 'Search' button and, in the **Search** dialogue, select the **Age** field.

2. Select the **less than ...** condition and type '16' in the search field at the foot of the dialogue.

3. Click on the **OK** button and the confirmation screen will appear with 'Age less than 16' highlighted.

4. Instead of clicking on the **Start Search** button, click the **And** button, to add another condition to the search. This time select the **Occupation** field from the drop-down list and **includes** as a search condition. Type 'servant' as the information to search for – the **includes** condition should locate any record with the word 'servant' in the occupation, but not, of course, terms, such as maid or butler.

5. Click the **OK** button and the confirmation screen will show: 'Age less than 16 and Occupation includes servant'. Click the **Start Search** button and all servants aged younger than 16 will be shown.

6. An answer to the question will be found by counting the records and further information could also be gleaned, e.g. were most young servants female?

Now show that some questions can be answered using the Graph tool. A good example is a question about occupations.

1. If using *Information Workshop*, click on the 'Graph' button on the toolbar – it shows a symbol of a small bar chart.

2. When the graphing screen opens, select a graph type from the buttons at the top – a vertical or horizontal bar chart is appropriate for displaying occupations in the census records. A dialogue box will open, from which you can select the **Occupation** field.

3. Click the **OK** button and the graph will appear on screen.

4. *Information Workshop* will count the frequency of terms in any field and display a frequency graph – not all software will do this, so if not using *Information Workshop*, you may need to amend your question.

5. Use the **Copy** command in the Graph window to copy the graph – it can then be pasted into a word processor to write a subsequent simple report of the enquiry.

Let the children choose questions to investigate in small groups. Emphasise that different questions will require different search techniques and the groups should be prepared to discuss and try out several possibilities. The groups will need support and monitoring during the activity – perhaps prompting to modify their question if searching proves fruitless. In a plenary at the end, get the groups to report back and summarise what they have found out about the locality in 1881. Focus again on how ICT has facilitated their investigations – how easily could they have found answers using the paper version of the census?

What should the children know already?

To get the most from this project, pupils need to be familiar with the idea of searching for information using ICT. If they have searched using a web-based tool (see Project 3), they should have the requisite knowledge and skills. The project needs to be set within the context of a study of everyday lives during the Victorian period, as required by the National Curriculum for history programme of study. During ICT Activity 2, some background knowledge will be required to enable pupils to put themselves into the roles required – for example, they will need to know about the role of servants in Victorian society and that children left school much earlier than now.

What do I need to know?

Where and how to obtain census data for the school's locality

The basic requirement for this project is access to census returns, known as enumerators' schedules, for one year in the late Victorian period. As already mentioned, local record office and archive services should be able to provide photocopies at a small cost. The National Archives, based at Kew, hold all original copies of Victorian census documents and have made some materials available online – see www. nationalarchives.gov.uk/teachers. The website of your local authority should provide information on record offices and archives in your area. You may be able to access relevant data on the FreeCEN website – http://freecen.rootsweb.com. This is a project aimed at making all nineteenth-century census documents available online through a searchable database. It is the work of volunteers with an interest in genealogy and family history. At the time of writing, it is far from complete, but data from some areas of the UK is available.

How to set up a database file

Once you have obtained your census documents, you then need to enter information into a database program, such as *Information Workshop*. Although the creation of a datafile with around 50 records seems quite daunting, it is a relatively straightforward process and should not take too long if you have reasonable keyboard skills. Using *Information Workshop*, follow these steps:

1. Start *Information Workshop* and select **Create a new file** on the first screen.
2. Select **Use the advanced file setup**, then click **Next**.
3. A dialogue box pops up. Enter your information about the datafile, for example:

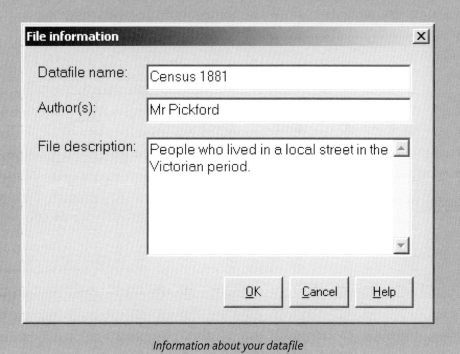

Information about your datafile

4. Click the **OK** button. The dialogue box disappears and is replaced by the one used to set the field headings.

5. Start by entering each of the headings you want to use.

6. Do this by clicking on the box under the **Fieldname** heading and typing 'House'.

7. Now press the down arrow (↓) key on the keyboard and type 'Name' in the next box. Keep working down the first column, until you have entered all the fieldnames for a late Victorian census – Relationship, Condition, Age, Occupation, Where Born.

8. You will have noticed that as you typed each name the word 'Words' appeared under the **Type** heading and 20 appeared under the **Size** heading. The other columns (**Units** and **Decimals**) should have remained blank at this time.

9. You need to change the **Type** heading for 'Age' to 'Numbers'. Move down to the **Type** box next to 'Age'. Click on the arrow in the **Type** box next to 'Age' and select 'Numbers'.

10. To enter the size of this field, move to the **Size** column, press the BACKSPACE key twice, and type '2'.

11. Return now to the **Type** box next to 'Condition'. You are going to change the type of information this field will hold.

12. Click on the down arrow next to the **Type** box and select 'Keywords'.

13. Click on the button to the far right that now has the word 'Keywords' on it. The **Keywords** dialogue box appears.

14. This box allows you to type in your keywords. It is best to use keywords in a field when you know the options are limited or you want to limit the choice. In this case type the following into the **New keyword** box: 'Married' and 'Unmarried'.

15. Press RETURN or click the **Add** button after each one. Click the **OK** button.

16. You may wish to change the **Size** attribute for your fields – it indicates the maximum number of characters (including spaces) that can be entered in a field.

Your finished setup should look like this:

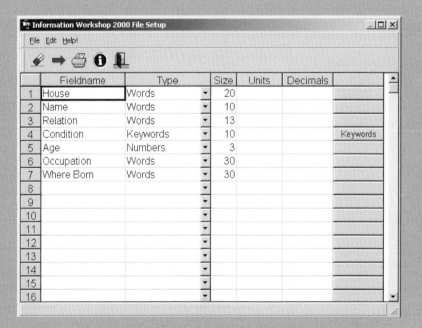

The Advanced File Setup *window*

When you have finished setting up the file, click the 'Quit' button (it looks like an open door). You are now ready to add records to your file. Because you have set up a new file, the program has 'pressed the Edit button' for you and you can start entering your information. A new, blank record sheet is displayed for you. Most of it will be yellow to remind you that you are changing a file. Add information and press RETURN to move from field to field. To add a new record use the **Add Record** command in the **Edit** menu. When you have finished, use the **Save File** button to save the datafile. To search, sort and graph from the datafile, you need to click the 'Edit' button on the toolbar (it has a pencil symbol). Your *Information Workshop* census datafile is now ready for classroom use.

If time is very restricted, a ready-made census database, with accompanying activities at varying levels of difficulty, is available on the Web. The Greenfield Road database can be explored online or downloaded from the Naace website (formerly MAPE) at www.mape.org.uk/activities/index.htm. It is a free-standing program, requiring no additional software, available for Windows PC and Macintosh OS 9. With some additional preparation, all of the activities in this project could be carried out using the Greenfield Road database. It has a well-structured approach to the development of advanced search techniques and contains information from several census years. Its disadvantage is that it does not have the local dimension of your own datafile, making the project less relevant and motivating for children.

What will the children learn?

As well as being a meaningful introduction to more advanced searching techniques and the capabilities of database software, the project will lead to high-quality learning in history. Children will be able to find answers to enquiry questions about real people who lived in their locality in the past. The role play will enable them to empathise with ordinary people from the Victorian period and also gain an insight into how a census was carried out. It places the learning objectives and key ideas of the relevant QCA ICT scheme units into a purposeful subject context. Discussion about the activities will raise points about the strengths and limitation of census data and thus the issues arising from data analysis – the census can only answer a limited number of questions with accuracy, e.g. the name of occupation, not what it entailed. The role play is particularly valuable in raising issues of reliability. A Victorian census was the product of human interaction and depended, to a great extent, on the diligence of the enumerator and the honesty of those being questioned. Children will learn some valuable lessons about the origins of data and, by implication, the reliability of statistics.

Challenging the more able and supporting the less able: modifying the project for older and younger pupils

More experienced or older pupils could be challenged in a number of ways. They could create the database themselves, using paper census documents, or add some records, to a partiallly completed database. They could work more independently when answering questions and developing search techniques, using a wider range of search conditions, e.g. 'not the same as . . .', 'begins with . . .', or 'not equal to . . .' They could experiment with the graphing tools, finding appropriate graph types to answer specific questions. They could be encouraged to look more closely and question the plausibility of the information in the census – most census documents contain evidence of possible inaccuracies, for example, the Church Street datafile (on the CD-ROM that accompanies this book) contains a household where the head, a retired minister, appears to have a daughter only 14 years younger than himself!

Less experienced or younger pupils will need more adult and peer support when developing search techniques. They could also work on the role play in small groups to provide mutual support – one member of the group could represent the Victorian person with others taking on the roles of researchers. A simpler database program could be used – BlackCat's *First Workshop* has fewer search options and a more limited range of graphs, but still retains much of the functionality of *Information Workshop*.

Why teach this?

The project is targeted on ICT National Curriculum KS2 PoS statements 1a, 1b and 1c, which states that children should be able 'to interpret information, to check it is relevant and reasonable and to think about what might happen if there were any errors or omissions'. It also provides an opportunity to discuss the advantages and disadvantages of using ICT to find things out, as required by the 'Reviewing, modifying and evaluating work as it progresses' strand of the ICT PoS.

The project turns essentially quite dry, dense and relatively inaccessible census documents into a lively, dynamic resource for drama and historical investigation. The role play provides a highly motivating introduction to the speed and functions of database software within a context of historical learning about the locality. The project will successfully deliver the three products of good information handling identified by Govier (1997). There will be new knowledge, development of ICT capability and also 'a deeper engagement with learning such that the children want to go on to find out more'.

Science Project 4 (*Branching databases*), *Arts* Project 7 (*Using a spreadsheet model*), *English* Project 5 (*Villains*) and *Maths* Project 6 (*Statistical investigations 1*) provide parallel activities with databases.

References and further reading

Govier, H. (1997) 'Making sense of information', *MicroScope Information Handling Special 1997*. Available online at www.mape.org.uk/curriculum/skills/ making_sense.htm.

GEOGRAPHY

Project Fact Card: Project 7: Link with a contrasting locality

Who is it for?

- 7- to 10-year-olds (NC Levels 2–4)

What will the children do?

As part of a comparative study of their home locality and a contrasting locality, pupils will create a set of images, which convey the character of their locality to an audience in a distant place. They will write an online commentary or 'blog' about the images and make comments about images provided by a twinned school. They will find answers to questions about their own locality and communicate them via the internet.

What do I need to know?

- The e-mail address and other contact details of a school in an appropriate contrasting locality
- How to save pictures from a digital camera to your computer and/or how to scan images and save them
- The functions and features of your chosen photo sharing or web blogging service, including how to upload images
- Health and safety issues related to the use of the internet by children

What should the children know already?

- How to enter and edit text in a word processor
- How to write using a word processor, with an awareness of audience
- How to access a web page using a web browser
- How to take a picture with a digital or disposable camera

What resources will I need?

- A digital camera and accompanying software
- A web browser to access a photo sharing or weblogging (blogging) service

What will the children learn?

- That ICT can be used to exchange information in text and image form
- That web applications can be used to facilitate a dialogue between users in different locations
- That an awareness of audience is important when communicating using the internet

How to challenge the more able

- Encourage pupils to create a blog more independently
- Develop and refine text with a greater awareness of audience

How to support the less able

- Provide pupils with the opporunity to make comments and identify questions, with adult support

Why teach this?

- The project is targeted on ICT NC KS2 PoS statements 3a and 3b.
- The project supports, augments and extends the content of QCA ICT Scheme of Work Units 3E and 4A.
- The project supports teaching and learning about contrasting localities as required by the geography National Curriculum and the QCA Geography Scheme of Work Units 10, 13 and 18.

Link with a contrasting locality

What will the children do?

The study of contrasting localities is central to geography in the National Curriculum at Key Stage 2. The requirements are structured so that pupils are encouraged to make continuous comparisons between the contrasting place and their own locality through a series of key questions. Using the programme of study (PoS) as a basis, these questions can be summarised, as follows:

- What is the place like? (3a)
- Where is it in relation to other places? (3b, 3c)
- Why is the place like it is? (3d)
- How is the place changing? (3e)
- How is it similar and different to other places? (3f)
- How is the place linked to other places? (3g)

Before and during a study of a contrasting place, pupils should consider the questions in relation to their own locality and consider how others might view the place where they live. ICT, and specifically web-based technologies, now enable pupils to raise these questions with people who live in a contrasting place and also gather their views and comments. This project makes use of 'blogging' facilities on the Web to facilitate online communication focusing on the characteristics of places. The ICT activities should be located in a broader study of a contrasting locality which makes use of other resources, e.g. atlases, reference books, maps, to find answers to the key geographical questions. Before the first activity, pupils should be introduced to their twinned school and given information about its pupils and their locality. For information on how to set up twinning arrangements, see the *What do I need to know?* section of this project.

Activity 1: An introduction to 'blogging'

Using a large screen and an internet-linked computer, show the pupils an example blog, which conveys an impression of a place. Explain that the blog contains both pictures and text about the place and has a facility to enable users to raise questions and make comments. Explain that you want the children to plan and design a blog that will convey an impression of their locality to children in the twinned school. The blog must contain a set of pictures (maximum about 10), which gives an accurate impression, and comments, which explain and add to the pictures. The children should work in groups to plan their blog – as part of the task, they should use a local map to plan a route around the locality that takes in all the locations, which will be photographed for the blog. They should also begin to write the comments that will accompany the pictures. Set the groups to work – they could use word processors on hand-held, laptop or desktop computers to draft their comments, but handwritten notes will suffice.

Depending on time and circumstances, you may choose to take the photographs as part of fieldwork in the locality, with children taking turns at using simple digital or disposable cameras. When the photographs have been taken, you will need to download them from the digital cameras onto an internet-linked computer or network drive. Alternatively, if you have used a film-based camera, you will need to use a scanner to turn them into image files.

Activity 2: Creating a blog

The structure of Activity 2 will depend to a great extent on the photo sharing or blogging service that you have decided to use. Some blogging services, e.g. www.21publish.com, have the facility for multiple users to create individual blogs under one account. Using such a service, you could allow individuals or groups to create their own blogs by uploading images and writing comments independently – the result would be a very large and, probably, quite confusing site for your twinned school to access. If you choose to create one blog for your class (a simpler and more manageable option), Activity 2 could be structured as a lesson with children choosing, uploading and adding comments to images while gathered as a group around an interactive whiteboard or internet-linked computer linked to projector and screen. You could focus pupils' thinking by using key questions, such as 'Does this image give a clear impression of what our locality is like?' or 'What would you need to write to explain this picture?' Alternatively, the blog could be assembled over a longer period using a classroom computer with groups of children 'blogging' on a rota basis. With this option, adult support and/or monitoring would be needed to avoid technical problems and to keep the children focused on the purposes of the task.

Activity 3: Responding to comments and questions

Depending on resources, Activity 3 could be organised as a lesson (or sequence of lessons) in an ICT suite or could be structured around the use of one or more classroom computers. Explain to the children that they are going to look at and add questions/comments to a blog created by children in the twinned school. Give the children an overview of the site, using a large screen, and then let the class look at the blog, making notes of any questions/comments they would want to make. Remind them of the key questions about places to which they should be finding answers.

In a mini-plenary, review the questions and comments the pupils have noted down and select some to be added to the twinned school's blog. To avoid problems of multiple access to the blog, get the children to enter their comments/questions one at a time using a single computer linked to a large screen. Once a few comments have been entered, explain to the children that they are now going to read and prepare responses to the questions and comments children from the twinned school have made on the class's blog. Get the pupils to log in to the blog and give time for them to read the comments and make notes of possible responses.

In a plenary, get the children to sort the comments on the blog. Some questions will be ones that the children could answer immediately. Others will require research. Some contributions to the blog will be observations and remarks, not questions. Make a list of responses and next steps.

To a large extent, Activity 3 is open-ended in that children could engage in a continuing series of online exchanges of questions, comments and information centred on the blogs. Given time constraints in the curriculum, however, a couple of exchanges would be more realistic. In a final plenary, focus children's attention on the key place-related questions and the answers that they have found out, as well as the process of using the blogs. Your questions could include:

⊙ What is the locality of the twinned school like?

⊙ What do you think the children in the twinned school think our locality is like?

⊙ How did using the blogs compare with other ways of gathering information about places?

What should the children know already?

The skills involved in using web-based communication tools are relatively straightforward. Providing children know about the basic features of a web browser and how to enter and edit text in a word processor, they should be able to easily access and contribute to a blog. Uploading images to a blog requires a more advanced set of skills, however, and most children will need some support with the process. Many children will be familiar with the functions of a camera, whether digital or disposable, but again, some children may need additional support. Children who have completed Projects 3, 4 and 5 should have the requisite skills for this project.

What do I need to know?

The e-mail address and other contact details of a school in an appropriate contrasting locality

The basic requirement for the success of this project is the setting up of a twinning link with a school in an appropriate contrasting locality, either in the UK or overseas. This can be done in a number of ways, but probably the simplest is to use a web-based twinning service. There are several available, all of which have a similar approach. After registering your school details (and following some simple confirmations and checks), you can search a database of schools that are seeking links. Usually, you can enter quite detailed search criteria to narrow down your search, e.g. a primary school with internet access in a rural part of south-west England or a nursery school in rural Kenya where English is the first language. Services include:

- IECC (Intercultural E-mail Classroom Connections) – www.iecc.org
  An organisation, based in the US, for facilitating e-mail links between schools around the world.
- ePALS – www.epals.com
  Described as 'the world's largest online classroom community', another US-based service with a very large database of schools.
- IPFS (The International Pen Friend Service) – www.ipfs.org
- Global Gateway – www.globalgateway.org.uk
  A UK-based worldwide twinning site, managed by the British Council.
- My Europe – http://myeurope.eun.org
  A project, funded by the European Commission, to 'help teachers raise their pupils' awareness of what it means to be a young citizen in Europe'. It features a forum where teachers can request links with partner schools in the European Union.
- BBC World Class – www.bbc.co.uk/worldclass
  A BBC site which includes an extensive list of school twinning services.

Having located and made contact with a link school, your next step will be to communicate your idea for the project. Teachers in your twin school may not have the technical skills, time or interest to engage with a photo sharing or blogging service, so the project may have to be modified at this stage. Providing they are willing to view and comment on your class's blog, the project can go ahead, but with a more restricted focus. Instead of exchanging questions and comments, the project will focus on outsiders' impressions and views of the school locality – a valuable perspective for children to experience. Questions and answers about the distant locality could still be exchanged, but using e-mail, rather than blogging technology. QCA ICT Scheme of Work Unit 3E: *E-mail* provides a structure for this kind of link.

How to save pictures from a digital camera to your computer and/or how to scan images and save them

As one of the key features of weblogs is the inclusion of images, alongside text messages, you will need to find out how to download images from a digital camera or scan printed photographs, ready for uploading to your chosen service. Camera and scanner manufacturers use different software packages for performing these tasks, but all have similar functions and features. In the case of digital cameras, most can be connected to a computer by a Universal Serial Bus (USB) connection. Once you have installed your camera software, following the manufacturer's instructions in an accompanying manual, you will be ready to transfer your images from the camera to the computer's hard drive.

The USB connector from a camera (left), ready to be inserted into a USB connector extension from a computer (right). The computer's USB connectors are often on the back of the case, so an extension, like the one shown, makes connection much more convenient

A digital camera connected to a computer via USB

Once the camera is connected, the associated software will usually load automatically on the computer to facilitate the downloading of the images. The screenshot below shows a sample screen; indicating that the computer has recognised a camera and downloading will soon begin.

iPhoto *for Macintosh is typical of image software for digital cameras.*
This screen appears as soon as a camera is connected to the computer via USB. Once the camera is loaded, clicking on the Import *button activates the transfer of images*

Once the images have been transferred, the camera software usually presents the images on screen and will have functions for simple editing, a slide show, printing or sending by e-mail

The functions and features of your chosen photo sharing or web blogging service, including how to upload images

Once the images have been transferred to your computer, you will be able to upload chosen files to a photo sharing service or blog. Before doing this, you may need to locate the files on your computer — it is not always obvious where the images have been stored. On a Windows PC, camera software usually uses the **My Pictures** folder in **My Documents** for storage and the files will be found there, perhaps in a folder labelled with the download date or the name of the software. On a Macintosh running OS X, the images will normally be found in the **Pictures** folder, which is accessible from any window in the Finder.

Scanning printed photographs from disposable film cameras is another possibility. Frankly, it is not a recommended option as the resulting images are likely be of inferior quality to digital camera images and scanning software can be very complicated and cumbersome to use. For good quality images, your scanner needs to be set at a high resolution setting, measured usually in dots per inch or dpi — perhaps 300 dpi or better for subsequent printing. For the Web, a setting of 72 dpi will do. If scanning of printed images is your chosen option, make sure you save the resulting files to an easily accessible location on your computer — the **My Pictures** or **Pictures** folders being the best choice.

The final step in setting up the project will be your selection and familiarisation with a chosen photo sharing or blogging service. Blogs (shortened from weblogs) are web-based publications, usually in diary form, in which users communicate, through text and images, information about their everyday lives or about themes or subjects. Photo sharing services are primarily websites where digital photographers can display their images, either to a wide audience or a restricted audience such as family and friends — most are run commercially and have options for printing the images that are stored. Although photo sharing sites and blogs began as quite different types of web-based applications, they have become increasingly similar in style — photo sites now provide options for text descriptions of images, and blogs are increasingly more visual in their nature and style.

For the purpose of this project, you need to find a site which is straightforward and safe for children to use. As already mentioned, www.21publish.com offers a comprehensive service (used by many US schools) for the creation of individual blogs by large groups of children. It has a fairly steep learning curve for the teacher, however, and may be too complex for all but the most enthusiastic blogger. There are a few other dedicated sites devoted to blogging in an educational context, e.g. www.weblogg-ed.com, but photo sharing sites probably make more promising tools for an image-based blog. There are far too many of these sites to provide a comprehensive listing — most commercial photographic companies have sites, aimed at promoting their printing services, with a free photo sharing option, e.g. www.bootsdigitalphotocentre.com, www.truprint.co.uk, www.kodakgallery.co.uk. An interesting and quite different service is offered by Flickr (www.flickr.com), part of the Yahoo! network. As well as a facility for creating a private photo page with a unique URL or web address, e.g. www.flickr. com/photos/castleschool, it allows images to be described and also 'tagged' with keywords. The site can be searched using these tags and users can add comments to your images very easily.

If you decide to use Flickr, you need to take the following simple steps:

1. Log on to the Flickr site using any web browser – the web address or URL is www.flickr.com.
2. Create an account for yourself or your school – the service is free and setting up an account is very straightforward.
3. You can decide at this stage whether you want your uploaded images to be public (open for anyone who visits the Flickr site) or private, with access limited to specified 'friends', e.g. only visitors from your twinned school.
4. When the account is set up, your photo page will have a unique web address, which can be communicated to your twinned school – the format is www.flickr.com/photos/username. If you have chosen to make your images private, use the **Your Contacts** page, to give your twinned school access – specify the e-mail address that they will use to log on.
5. You are now ready to transfer your image files to the Flickr site. This can be done in one of two ways: either use the web page for uploading images on the site or download the *Flickr Uploadr* program to your computer. The *Uploadr* is a small software package for Windows and Macintosh which quickly transfers individual images or batches of images to your photo page.

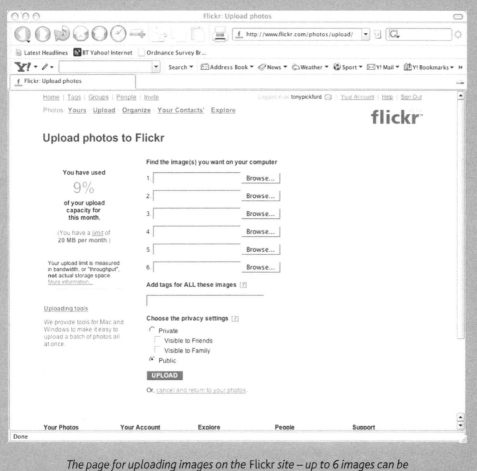

The page for uploading images on the Flickr site – up to 6 images can be uploaded at any one time. Use the Browse . . . buttons to locate images on your computer and click the UPLOAD button to transfer. Note that you can specify whether images will be public or private at this stage

Flickr Uploadr for Macintosh *has a simple interface (the* Windows *software is identical in function and layout)*

6. If using *Flickr Uploadr*, select the **Add Photos ...** command from the **Upload** menu and navigate to the **My Pictures** or **Pictures** folder to find your images. Select the image to be transferred and click on the **Open** button. At this point, if the image file is large, the software presents a window asking if you want to resize the image. To save on transfer time, it is advisable to resize the image to a size suitable for on-screen viewing.

The Uploadr *software suggests an appropriate size for on-screen viewing*

*Before uploading your image, you can add information in text form,
including 'Tags' or keywords to categorise it*

7. At this point, you can add information to the image in the form of a title, description and 'Tags', or keywords, to categorise it. Click the **Upload** button to transfer your image to your page on the Flickr website.

*Once it has been transferred, you can change the title, description and
Tags before moving your image to your 'Photos' page*

Images are displayed on your Flickr page with title, your description and the option to add comments. They can be deleted here, too – this option is obviously only available to you, as the page's owner!

8. When the transfer is complete, *Flickr Uploadr* brings up a dialogue box asking if you want to open the photo on the site. Click the **Open** Flickr button and your web browser will display a confirmation page, where final checks can be made on the text that you have added (see the screenshot on p. 79). Click **OK** to confirm.

9. The images on your photo page can be viewed in a number of ways: as small images on one page, individually at full size or as a slide show.

10. You (and children from the twinned school) can add comments to any accessible image on the Flickr site. Click on the **Comments** hyperlink below an image and a page will open, showing the photo at a larger size, with a text entry box. When text has been entered, in the form of a comment, question or response, click on the **Post Comment** button to confirm. The page owner can access any comments by clicking on the **Comments** hyperlink for a picture – the number of comments is indicated beneath each image.

Health and safety issues related to the use of the internet by children

Flickr is an incredibly rich resource with options for grouping, organising and categorising images in a number of ways – the steps indicated above merely 'scratch the

The Comments *page for an image in* Flickr *– if your image is categorised as 'public', this is accessible to anyone viewing the site. If your images are 'private', comments can only be made by your specified Contacts*

surface' of what is possible. The tagging of images, in itself, has opened up a new paradigm in the way in which images are searched and viewed. Flickr is constantly checked and monitored by Yahoo! and its users. However, as a public site, with constantly changing content, there is always a remote possibility that images or comments can appear which you might consider unsuitable for your children. For this reason, pupils do need to be supervised when viewing the site (as is the case with any web-based activity) and images should be accessed using the full web address – www.flickr.com/photos/username – not just www.flickr.com. Setting up your photo page as a 'private' resource will ensure that comments about images are only made by your specified contacts.

What will the children learn?

The project has tremendous potential for learning. The process of blogging – selecting images, writing explanations, adding comments, responding to questions – brings the exchange of information using ICT to life in a way that is not possible with e-mail. Information in visual and written form can be closely integrated and the comments of the audience become part of the blog, not a separate response. Children can modify their blog in response to the audience's needs and develop a deeper appreciation of how their work is viewed by others.

The project will greatly enhance children's geographical understandings. If they have access to a blog from a twinned school, they will begin to find answers to that most difficult of geographical questions about a contrasting locality: 'What do the people who live there feel about the place where they live?' Even without a blog from a contrasting locality, the project has great value because the comments and questions of others will provide new perspectives on their own locality.

Challenging the more able and supporting the less able: modifying the project for older and younger pupils

Depending on the chosen photo sharing or weblogging service, more experienced pupils could be stretched by allowing them to work more independently. If this is not an option, then more experienced pupils could be given the role of group leaders when designing a blog or when responding to comments. They could be encouraged to write in more depth about their own locality with greater sensitivity to the needs of the audience. Their blog could focus on a specific theme or aspect of the locality – possibly a blog which presents the locality as a tourist destination or one which focuses on jobs and employment.

If working independently, less experienced pupils will need more adult or other support when dealing with the technical aspects of blogging – browsing for files on the computer, transferring images, editing text. They will also benefit from more in-depth discussion about their audience. Responding to questions and comments from real people in a twinned school is a particularly good way of bringing a contrasting locality study to life for younger children.

Why teach this?

The project provides an excellent opportunity to discuss the strengths and weaknesses of the use of ICT for communicating information as required by the 'Reviewing, modifying and evaluating work as it progresses' strand of the ICT PoS. It extends and updates the content of QCA ICT Scheme of Work Units 3E: *E-mail* and 4A: *Writing for different audiences*, moving them into new, highly relevant areas. A dialogue of questions and responses is a particularly effective way of learning how to write for a specific audience. Blogging exploits the potential of the internet as a tool for multimedia communication, much more effectively than e-mail. Although research into the educational impact of blogging is limited at the moment, there are indications that it can have a powerful and profound effect on learning. When writing about the potential of ICT for mixing media, such as text and images, to create meaning, David Wray (2001) states that ICT tools make information 'readily changeable to meet different purposes and audiences – information is always provisional and open to alteration'. Graham Lewis (2005) goes further and states: 'blogs and associated technologies could well be the "killer app" that allows us to deliver the long overdue promise of the internet to support more constructivist, student centred, higher order learning'.

See *Learning ICT in English* Project 6 (*Imaginative e-mail*) and Project 7 (*Photo-dramas*) for related activities.

References and further reading

Lewis, G. (2005) 'Can blogs be useful educational tools?' Centre for Academic Practice, University of Warwick. Available online at www.warwick.ac.uk/services/cap

Wray, D. (2001) 'Using ICT to enhance literacy'. Available online at www.warwick.ac.uk/staff/D.J.Wray/Articles/ictlit.pdf

HISTORY

Project Fact Card: Project 8: Making an information source

Who is it for?

- 9- to 11-year-olds (NC Levels 2–5)

What will the children do?

Organise and communicate information about a chosen period chronologically. Use a multimedia authoring program to refine and present information in different forms for a specific audience. Use more complex searches to locate information.

What should the children know already?

- How to copy and paste information in text/graphic form from one application to another
- How to refine a search using a web-based search tool using simple strategies

What do I need to know?

- The location (URLs) of search tools for images and sounds
- How to configure a 'safe search' on a chosen web search page
- How to copy images from a web browser to a multimedia authoring program
- How to save sounds from a web search page and insert them into a multi-media authoring program
- Functions of a chosen multimedia authoring program

What resources will I need?

- A multimedia authoring program, which can be used to present information in linear form, e.g. *Microsoft PowerPoint* or *Timelines*

What will the children learn?

- To search for images and sounds on the Web using simple and more complex search strategies
- To insert images and sounds into a multimedia authoring program
- To use a multimedia authoring program to refine and present information in different forms for a specific audience
- To compare the presentation of information with multimedia to presentation by paper-based means

How to challenge the more able

- Require a more extended time scale for the timeline or increase the requirement for detail in the text of the presentation
- Use a more sophisticated multimedia authoring program that has the facility to display video and/or animations
- Set a more challenging audience for the presentation, e.g. Y7 pupils in a neighbouring secondary school

How to support the less able

- Use a simpler multimedia authoring program
- Provide a set of images and sounds on disk for children to choose from
- Provide more structure and guidance to support work with the multimedia authoring program, e.g. a ready-prepared template for pupils to use

Why teach this?

- The project is targeted on ICT NC KS2 PoS statements 1a, 1b, 2a and 3b.
- It supports and augments the content of QCA ICT Scheme of Work Units 6A and 6D.
- The project helps pupils to organise and communicate historical information, as required by the history PoS statements 5a, 5b and 5c.
- The project could be used to help children to communicate their knowledge and understanding in several contexts within the QCA history scheme of work, specifically Units 12, 13 and 20.

Making an information source

What will the children do?

This project should be used to conclude pupils' enquiries about a particular historical period or the life of a significant historical figure. Having researched using a range of sources, pupils should have gathered information in response to enquiry questions (mainly in handwritten or word-processed text form) and be ready to present this information to an audience. ICT is used here to help pupils to organise this information chronologically and to present it in an engaging and cogent manner.

Activity 1: Creating a timeline

Gather the pupils around a large screen. Ask key questions to remind pupils about the historical period/person they have been studying and the enquiry questions that they have been answering. Make a point that the information they have found could be presented to an audience in lots of ways, e.g. a wall display, a whole-school assembly or a newsletter, but, as the information they have gathered is about changes/events/developments over a period of time, an appropriate form of presentation is a timeline. Explain that they are going to record the information on an on-screen timeline that an audience can explore independently. At this point, give children information on their intended audience, e.g. parents, younger children or children in a parallel class.

Demonstrate the software – the ideal software for this project is *Timelines*, produced by SoftTeach (www.soft-teach.co.uk) (a demo is available on the CD), but another multimedia authoring program could be used (see the 'What do I need to know?' section). Show how the timeline is set up and how to enter information in text form, e.g. in *Timelines*, information is placed in information boxes which are brought up on screen when symbols on the timeline are clicked. Explain that, to begin, the pupils should enter information in text form at appropriate points on the timeline, e.g. if it is a timeline of a person's life, then information about date and place of birth will be an appropriate starting point followed by information at key points in the person's life. Explain that you want the children to show what they have learned and can recall about the period or person, so the text should be their own work – they will be working in small groups and should collaborate on the writing. By the end of this first activity, they should have entered information at at least six points on the timeline – more, if possible. They should be especially careful to locate the dates of events accurately.

Pupils should then be given time to set up and add information to their timelines. During this group activity, prompt the children to explain why they have chosen to put particular events on their timelines. Why is the event important/significant? Also prompt them to save their file at regular intervals.

In a plenary, ask children to report back on the events they have selected and why. Also ask them how the timeline on screen is different to a timeline on paper or on a wall display.

Activity 2: Adding information in the form of images

At the start of the second session, gather the pupils around a large screen and remind them about the first activity. The screen needs to be linked to a networked computer with internet access. Show a sample timeline produced by one of the groups in the first session and point out that the information is at present only in text form. Explain that in this session, the children are going to enhance their timelines by adding information in the form of images and, later, sounds.

Open a web browser window and show the chosen Image Search tool on the Web – e.g. Google Images: http://images.google.co.uk. Demonstrate how to locate an image by typing words in the search box and also how to use the Advanced Image Search to locate appropriate images more precisely. Demonstrate how to select and copy an image.

Open the multimedia authoring program and demonstrate how to insert an image to go alongside the text already created. The text may now need to be amended, e.g. to explain what the image shows. Explain that you want children to find appropriate images for all the information boxes they have created. Also make the point that, for copyright reasons, they need to acknowledge in their text where the image came from, e.g. www.bbc.co.uk or http://tudorhistory.org.

Set the pupils off on this activity – again collaborating and taking turns in groups. With a teaching assistant, if available, monitor the groups carefully to ensure no unsuitable images are searched for or found – if *SafeSearch* is set up on Google Images this should not be a problem (see the 'What do I need to know?' section). Also prompt pupils to save their files at regular intervals.

In a plenary, ask children to report back on what they have achieved so far and, if possible, show some example timelines to the class. Again, get them to compare their on-screen timeline to a paper-based one or wall display.

Activity 3: Adding information in the form of sounds

At the start of the third session, gather the pupils around a large screen and remind them about the activities so far. The screen needs to be linked to a networked computer with internet access. Show a sample timeline produced by one of the groups in the first and second sessions and point out that the information is at present only in text and image form. Explain that in this session, the children are going to enhance their timelines by adding information in the form of sounds. The sounds may be directly relevant to the information, e.g. a sound file of a historical person speaking or singing, or could be short sound effects to enhance the user's experience. Remind children about the audience for their presentation.

Open a web browser window and show the chosen Sounds Search tool on the Web – e.g. www.findsounds.com for sound effects. Demonstrate how to locate a sound by typing words in the search box and also how to select an appropriate file format, e.g. .WAV. Demonstrate how to download and save a sound. As well as sound effects, some websites are available with archives of appropriate sounds, particularly for the Britain since 1930 period (e.g. www.hants.gov.uk/record-office/sound) from Hampshire Record Office has two short sound files of Sir Winston Churchill's voice.

Open the multimedia authoring program and demonstrate how to insert a sound to go alongside the text and images already set up. Explain that you want children to find appropriate sounds for some of the information boxes that they have created, but not all. Also explain that this is the final session they will be working on their timelines, so they should check all the information carefully for accuracy and make any final changes to the presentation.

In a plenary, ask children to report back on what they have achieved and, if possible, show some example timelines to the class. Again, get them to compare their on-screen timeline to a paper-based one or wall display. How could they develop or improve their timeline to make it even more appropriate for the audience?

What should the children know already?

Project 5, *Repurposing information for different audiences,* and/or QCA ICT Scheme of Work Unit 4A: *Writing for different audiences* cover the prior learning required for this project. Providing pupils know (a) how to copy and paste information in text/graphic form from one application to another and (b) how to refine a search using a web-based search tool, they should be able to engage with this project satisfactorily.

What do I need to know?

The location (URLs) of search tools for images and sounds

Many web-based search tools, for example Google (www.google.co.uk) and Lycos (www.lycos.co.uk) offer the facility to search for images as well as text. Searching for sound files can also be accomplished using these tools, but specialist sites, such as www.findsounds.com, provide a more comprehensive, dedicated service. If you are using the *Timelines* program, you will need to restrict the search to .WAV sound files only (as this is the only file format the software will accept); on the first page of the www.findsounds.com website, simply uncheck the .AIFF and .AU checkboxes.

How to configure a 'safe search' on a chosen web search page

Unless you are using a 'child' or 'family friendly' search, e.g. BBCi (www.bbc.co.uk), you will need to configure the search tool to ensure that it does not find unsuitable results. Most school networks should have software installed to block unsuitable sites, but, as such software is not foolproof and, sometimes, is not maintained effectively, it is better to be safe than sorry.

The process for configuring 'safe searches' varies from search tool to search tool.

⊙ On Lycos, click on the **Advanced Search** link on the home page and make sure that the 'Family Filter' is switched on – click the **Yes** radio button next to the question: 'Show family safe pages only?'

⊙ Using Google, select **Preferences** on the home page and click the radio button next to 'Use strict filtering' in the **SafeSearch Filtering** section of the **Preferences** page.

⊙ In Ask Jeeves (www.ask.co.uk) – a popular site, because it responds to natural language questions – you will need to select **Settings** in the top R.H. corner of the home page and click the radio button next to 'minimise adult content in search results and do not show an alert' in the **Content filtering** section of the preferences.

⊙ Using AltaVista (www.altavista.co.uk), select **Settings** on the home page and, in the **Family Filter** preferences, click the radio button next to '**All** – filters all searches: web pages, images, audio and video'.

It is important to note that the 'safe searches' that can be carried out using these tools will effectively block content from 'adult' sites, but will not block content from other sites containing unsuitable material, e.g. political propaganda, satirical sites or parodies which may give quite erroneous impressions.

How to copy images from a web browser to a multimedia authoring program

If using the *Timelines* program, images can be very easily copied from a web page into an information box on a timeline: simply right click on the chosen image in the web page and select **Copy** from the contextual menu. In *Timelines*, open the relevant information box and select **Paste** in the **Picture** sub-menu of the **Edit** menu – the copied picture will be pasted into the information box. Alternatively, a picture can be saved to a computer's hard disk and then imported into an information box using **Import > Picture** in the **File** menu.

How to save sounds from a web search page and insert them into a multimedia authoring program

It is not possible, unfortunately, to simply **copy** and **paste** sounds into a *Timelines* information box. Once an appropriate sound file has been located on a website, you will need to right click on the link to the file and select **Save Target As . . .** from the contextual menu. Just as with a picture, save the file to the computer's hard disk (the Desktop or the **My Documents** folder on a Windows PC) and then import into an information box using **Import > Sound** in the **File** menu.

Functions of a chosen multimedia authoring program

Timelines offers a range of functions to enable chronological information to be stored and retrieved. Once a scale and time period has been set up on a timeline, events and spans of time can be added by dropping icons from the key at the right-hand side of the screen. Once an icon has been dragged and dropped, a dialogue box appears into which a date, title and type of event can be entered. Further information can then be entered into the information box which appears when the icon is double clicked. Once information has been entered, the timeline can be locked to prevent changes by another user – there is a clear symbol resembling a padlock in the toolbar at the top of the screen. A user cannot then change the timeline, but can zoom in and out, scroll through the events (using direction arrows on the right and left of the screen) and search. The program will search for specific dates, key symbols and words in the title of events.

The main window of the Timelines *program showing the timeline and the key containing symbols*

Other multimedia authoring programs could be used to convey chronological information. A linear presentation program, such as *Microsoft PowerPoint*, could show a sequence of events on a series of screens. A non-linear tool, such as *HyperStudio* (TAG Learning), could be configured to show information on on-screen 'cards' linked to a timeline in graphic form on an initial screen. Such programs would require some initial structuring by the teacher. Setting up a template file would reduce the initial steep learning curve required by such programs.

What will the children learn?

Searching for images and sounds requires slightly different skills to purely text-based searches. As web search tools cannot 'read' pictures and sounds, they actually search in the text descriptions given by web page authors to images and sounds. Such text descriptions (alternative or ALT text) are rarely lengthy, so children will soon learn that natural language questions and lengthy, highly specific search terms yield few results. For example, 'King Alfred burning the cakes' will produce no results when searching using the Google Images search tool. 'King Alfred cakes', however, produces 45 results – some of which being images of a particular kind of fungus that bears this name. Several images, however, are entirely apposite, being pictures of statues of the king, or artists' impressions of the story.

Many multimedia authoring programs, including *Timelines* and *PowerPoint*, support the copying and pasting of images from other programs, such as web browsers. Although this is, by far, the easiest way of transferring and inserting images, the routine of saving images and sounds as separate files for insertion into other programs is a useful set of skills for children to learn.

An awareness of the audience and their interests and needs is important in a range of curriculum contexts – for example, writing for specific audiences is a core aspect of the English curriculum. In the context of electronic media, children need to be aware of simple design ideas, e.g. keeping on-screen text relatively brief and choosing images and sounds which complement and do not detract from the text. *Timelines* allows far fewer choices in terms of presentation than *PowerPoint*. Although, in some ways, this is a shortcoming, the restricted functions enable children to focus more effectively on the information to be conveyed and how to make it accessible to the potential audience. Research suggests that, in some contexts, the animations and effects offered by *PowerPoint* can distract attention from the real purpose of communication. In his survey of computer use in US schools, Pflaum (2004: 192) remarks, in relation to *PowerPoint*, that he saw pupils' 'thought and energy going into exploring the mechanics of the software instead of the content being studied'.

Discussion during and at the end of the project should focus on comparisons between paper-based and electronic forms of communication. Key questions should focus on the effectiveness of the different forms of communication for conveying information clearly. If possible, evaluations from the presentation's audience should be fed into the discussion.

Challenging the more able and supporting the less able: modifying the project for older and younger pupils

Older or more skilled pupils could be challenged in a number of ways. In the context of the subject, a more extended time scale for the timeline would require more extensive research, perhaps from a wider range of sources. More detail could be required in the text of the presentation or, more usefully, greater refinement of the text to identify key points and key ideas. Pupils could be given a more challenging audience for the presentation – for example, Y7 pupils from a local secondary school who might already know something about the person or period being presented. More able pupils could be presented with a more sophisticated multimedia authoring program with the facility to display video and/or animations. Although such a program might offer greater potential for distraction from the main task, more skilled pupils could devise appropriate on-screen effects or include video clips which add to the audience's experience. A presentation on a person, time-frame or issue from the recent past might be enhanced by inclusion of appropriate video clips from the British Pathe archive, available on the Web – www.britishpathe.com.

Younger and/or less able pupils could be supported in a number of ways. A simpler multimedia authoring program could be provided (e.g. *2Create* from 2Simple Software) or a pre-prepared template could be set up, into which children enter information in text and picture form – a *Timelines* file with blank, or partially completed, information boxes would be appropriate for this purpose. Alternatively, pupils could be provided with a set of images and sounds on disk. Although this would negate the need to search on the Web (and thus not meet some of the intended learning objectives for the activity), it would still require pupils to select suitable media and place items in appropriate places in their presentation.

Why teach this?

The project supports and augments the content of QCA ICT Scheme of Work Units 6A: *Multimedia presentation* and 6D: *Using the internet to search large databases and to interpret information*, by focusing on search techniques to find non-text-based information and by setting the presentation of information into a chronological context. The presentation of information chronologically is a particularly appropriate approach for QCA History Scheme of Work Unit 12: *How did life change in our locality in Victorian times?*, Unit 13: *How has life in Britain changed since 1948?* and Unit 20: *What can we learn about recent history from studying the life of a famous person?*.

Research suggests that this type of project will develop cross-curricular ICT skills and contribute to the development of greater knowledge and understanding in subject contexts. Moseley and Higgins *et al.* (1999) report on a project in a Y4 classroom in which children created multimedia presentations to teach other pupils about the correct use of omissive apostrophes. Not only were children's understandings greatly improved by the process (as shown by improved test scores), it also helped the teacher to 'appreciate the children's difficulties and use that knowledge to improve their understanding'. Children used the provisionality of ICT to make rapid and dynamic changes, thus improving their presentation for the intended audience. The result was the development of enhanced ICT skills and the achievement of learning objectives in a complex and 'difficult' area of literacy.

Cooper (2000) reports on several projects in which pupils used ICT to enhance their organisation and communication of historical knowledge and understandings. Although none involved the use of more complex multimedia software, one project allowed pupils in Y5/6 to use a combination of images and text to convey their understandings of different viewpoints on the Spanish Armada. Broadsheet 'newspapers' were produced giving French, Spanish, English Protestant, English Catholic and Dutch viewpoints. The use of ICT motivated the children and gave them experience of communicating understandings in the form of 'press releases' for different audiences. Again, the ability to make rapid changes contributed positively to the learning and allowed for continuous evaluation and re-evaluation of the information and its presentation.

Although in a Key Stage 3 context, a study by Brown and Purvis (2001) is particularly significant for this project in that it stresses the particular appropriateness of multimedia in the context of history, in that it enables pupils 'to support their findings in a more sophisticated way, by the ease of incorporating evidence into their work'. The study also points out that the use of multimedia software can help to develop 'a culture of pupils as teachers as well as learners' (ibid.). There will be times during a multimedia-based project when pupils will need to show peers and the teacher new skills and techniques they have learned. Although this shift in roles may not be a comfortable experience for the teacher, it can have great benefit for pupils in fostering their autonomy, self-esteem and confidence.

See also *Learning ICT in English* Project 4 (*Working with audio*), *Science* Project 7 (*Multimedia information source*) and *Science* Project 10 (*Using search engines*) for related activities.

References and further reading

Brown, L. and Purvis, R. (2001) 'What is the impact of multisource learning on History at Key Stage 3?' Technology-integrated Pedagogical Strategies (TiPS) Project Case Studies, University of Cambridge, Faculty of Education. Available online at www.educ.cam.ac.uk/TiPS/reports.html

Cooper, H. (2000) *The Teaching of History in Primary Schools: Implementing the Revised National Curriculum* (3rd edn). London: David Fulton Publishers.

Hodkinson, A. (2001) 'Enhancing temporal cognition: practical activities for the primary classroom', *Primary History*, May, 28, 11–14.

Moseley, D. and Higgins, S. *et al.* (1999) 'Ways forward with ICT: effective pedagogy using information and communications technology for literacy and numeracy in primary schools'. University of Newcastle and CEM Centre, Durham University.

Available online at www.ncl.ac.uk/ecls/research/project_ ttaict/ttaict3.htm

Pflaum, W. (2004) *The Technology Fix: The Promise and Reality of Computers in Our Schools*. Alexandria, VA: Association for Supervision and Curriculum Development (ASCD).

RELIGIOUS EDUCATION

Project Fact Card: Project 9: A video of a visit to a place of worship

Who is it for?

- 9- to 11-year-olds (NC Levels 2–5)

What will the children do?

Following a visit to a place of worship, during which images have been made using a digital camera, pupils will create a short video sequence as a record of the visit. They will use images, audio and text to convey an impression of the place to an audience.

What should the children know already?

- How to use a digital camera
- How to view and rename files on the computer

What do I need to know?

- The functions of a simple digital video package, e.g. *QuickTime Player Pro, Windows Movie Maker*
- How to add audio and text using a simple video editing package

What resources will I need?

- Digital cameras and a simple video editing package, e.g. *Windows Movie Maker or QuickTime Player Pro*

What will the children learn?

- To assemble a short digital video using still images, audio and text
- To convey an impression of a place of worship, focusing on its character and symbolism

How to challenge the more able

- Use more sophisticated features of a digital video package, including transitions, titles and effects
- Assemble and edit a package, using moving images from a digital video camera
- Convey an impression of a more unfamiliar or distant place of worship, using images from an external source, such as an image library

How to support the less able

- Pre-prepare and order image and appropriate audio files for assembly into a video sequence
- Provide more adult or peer support during the process

Why teach this?

- The project is targeted on ICT NC KS1 PoS statements 2a, 3a and 3b.
- The project augments and extends the content of QCA ICT Scheme of Work Unit 6A.
- Visits to places of worship are a key element of the programme of study for KS2 in the QCA national framework for religious education and the QCA religious education scheme of work.

A video of a visit to a place of worship

What will the children do?

Although the ICT activities in this project could be completed using visual images taken by others, the project is likely to be most effective if children have been involved in the creation of the images. A necessary precursor to the ICT work, therefore, will be the organisation of a visit to a local place of worship. In the following description of the activities, reference is made to aspects of a Christian church, but another place of worship could be visited. It should be noted that some places of worship may put restrictions on the taking of photographs and, as noted in Project 4, in places where a chosen faith community is small, a whole-class visit could be inconvenient and an imposition. Prior to and during the visit, prompt children to identify the key locations in the place of worship, e.g. the altar, and point out symbols that are of importance in the chosen faith. A single, shared digital camera could be used to take the photographs, with locations being identified by group discussion during the visit. Several digital cameras would give children more choice and flexibility, but might complicate the later work, simply because of an over-abundance of images. Make sure children are aware that the images are being created for later use in a presentation recording their visit, which may be seen by parents and members of the chosen faith community. It should include images of the outside, as well as the inside of the building.

On your return from the visit, images will need to be downloaded to a computer or, in an ICT suite, a network server. If several cameras have been used and you are downloading to multiple computers, to be used by several groups, it could be a lengthy process. Technical information about downloading images from a digital camera is provided in Project 7.

Activity 1: Making a video from a sequence of images

In an introduction, ask questions and provide prompts to enable children to identify the purpose of their visit. Show some of the pictures taken by the children on screen and, through questioning, get the children to identify the key locations and symbols that they saw. Explain that you want the children to work in small groups on a short video which gives an impression of the place of worship, in particular conveying the character and atmosphere of the building, Show the children how to create a short digital video sequence, using still images, with your chosen software. Play the sequence and ask children for feedback, especially on the order of the images. Show the children how to change the order of the images and play the video through again. Explain that later the children will be able to add a soundtrack and text to the video, but for the moment, they should focus on the visuals. Set the children to work in small groups. Your interventions during the independent work should focus on making sure that children are including key aspects of the place of worship in their video, as well as helping with any technical issues.

In a plenary, show a sample of the saved videos to the children. Get them to identify the strengths and weaknesses of the samples – particularly focusing on how well the sequences reflect their experience of the visit and the atmosphere of the place of worship. Ask them to think about the music that they might use to accompany the visuals.

Your next step will depend on the type of music you want the children to add to their videos – before the next activity, you may want children to create and record their own music or you may want to assemble a collection of appropriate music tracks from which they can choose.

Activity 2: Adding a soundtrack

Gather children around a large screen and show a sample of the videos again to remind them of the process completed so far. Explain that you want the children to add music and text to their videos in this session. Discuss with the children what the most appropriate type of music might be. Play a selection of the possible music tracks and get children to comment on their appropriateness. Demonstrate how to add an audio track to the video, using your chosen software.

Ask children about possible text they might want to add to their video. Some captions may be appropriate, labelling parts of the building, e.g. the spire, font, etc. At the very least, children should add a title to the video. Set the children to work on the task of adding audio and text. Provide support and prompts, where necessary. Save the videos at the end of the process.

Activity 3: Adding text and titles

The final activity could form a plenary to Activity 2, if time allows, or could be a separate activity. Explain to the children that you want them to write a short review of a video created by another group. The review should focus on how well they feel the video conveys an impression of the place of worship. Stress to the children that the review should be positive and supportive. They should suggest improvements and ways of developing the video. Provide the children with a structure for the review in the form of a paper or on-screen writing frame. Questions and starting points for the review could include:

⊙ Does the video show the outside of the place of worship clearly?

⊙ Does the video feature all the important parts of the church?

⊙ Does the music create the right atmosphere? Does it fit in with the visuals?

⊙ Are the titles clear?

Set the groups to work and encourage them to view the video under review several times before making judgements and comments. In a plenary, share the videos and accompanying reviews with the class. As a class, consider whether their videos have done justice to the place of worship. Would the videos be a good substitute for a visit? You could share the videos with another class (who have not made a visit) to get an 'unbiased' view.

What should the children know already?

Familiarity with the controls of your chosen digital camera is a basic requirement for the project. The other prerequisite skills depend, to a great extent, on your chosen video editing package. Although it is otherwise a simple video editing package, Apple's *QuickTime Player Pro* requires some knowledge of how to rename and reorder files. Other editors, e.g. Microsoft *Windows Movie Maker,* Apple *iMovie* and Digital Blue *Digital Movie Creator*, allow reordering of images, using drag and drop, within the interface of the program.

What do I need to know?

The functions of a simple digital video package, e.g. *QuickTime Player Pro, Windows Movie Maker*

To teach this project, you need be familiar with the editing functions of a chosen video editing package. Your choice of package will depend on several factors. Price may be a significant consideration. Some packages, e.g. *Windows Movie Maker* and *iMovie HD*, are free, in the sense that they are installed on all Windows XP and Macintosh OS X computers. Others, e.g. Digital Blue *Digital Movie Creator* or *ArcSoft VideoImpression*, are bundled with some digital cameras. A more fundamental consideration, however, is the extent to which you want children to focus on technical aspects of video creation, possibly at the expense of subject learning – do you want children to spend time discussing transitions and effects or do you want them to focus on the content of the video and how well it conveys an impression of the place of worship? Do you want them to talk about 'wipes' and 'dissolves' or the best images to convey the stillness and grandeur of a church? You may say that you want both. I would argue that the 'bells and whistles' of some editing packages may get in the way of subject learning. For this reason, the focus of this section is *QuickTime Player Pro* – a package which does not offer the transitions and effects of some packages, but does the job of video creation quickly and effectively. *QuickTime Player* for Windows PC or Macintosh can be downloaded from www.quicktime.com. A site licence for a primary school, which activates the video editing features, is relatively inexpensive. The screenshots below show the Windows version of *QuickTime Player Pro*.

To create a video from a sequence of images, follow these steps:

1. Start *QuickTime Player Pro* and select **Open Image Sequence...** form the **File** menu.
2. Navigate to the folder on disk containing the images that you want to use – *QuickTime* reads a range of image formats, including the JPEG format used by most digital cameras. Click on the first image file in the **Open** dialogue box window.

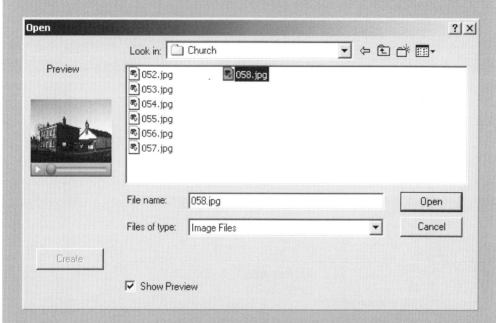

The Open *dialogue box window*

3. Click **Open** and the image files will be imported. A dialogue then appears in which you can choose the frame rate – how long each image will appear on screen. Select an appropriate time, e.g. 5 seconds per frame.

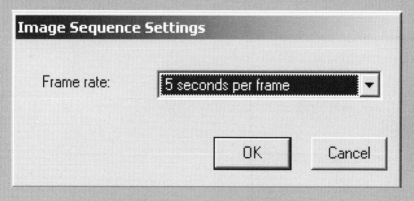

The Image Sequence Settings *dialogue*

4. Click **OK**. Your video sequence will now appear on screen with the first image in the sequence in view. Click on the **Play/Pause** button to play the video.

5. Select **Save As . . .** from the **File** menu to save the file as a *QuickTime* movie (.mov) file.

If, after viewing the video, you want to change the order of the images, you will need to change their file names and then repeat the process described above to create a new video sequence.

QuickTime Player Pro uses the file names of images to determine their sequence. Images will appear according the alphabetical or numerical order in a folder. To change the order, you need to open the folder in which the image files are stored and change their file names – naming them 001.jpg, 002.jpg, 003.jpg, etc. is simplest.

In Windows, open the image files folder and then right click on an image you wish to rename. Select **Rename** from the resulting menu. The file name will become high-lighted and you can type in a new name. Press RETURN to confirm.

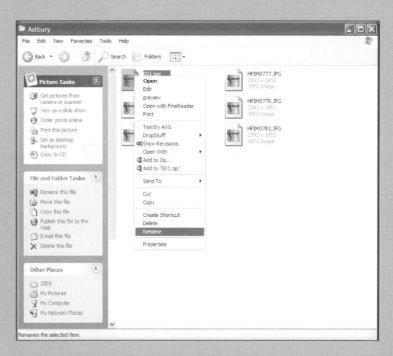

*Right clicking on a file and selecting **Rename** from the contextual menu is one way of renaming a file in Windows*

In Macintosh OS X, open the folder containing image files and click once on the file name that you want to change. The name will become highlighted and you can type in a new name. Press RETURN to confirm.

How to add audio and text using a simple video editing package

To add an audio file, follow these steps:

1. Open your *QuickTime* movie and make a note of its length – click on the **Go to End** button and the **Playback head** will move to the end of the movie and show its

The QuickTime *movie controller*

length in hours, minutes and seconds (it is highly unlikely that your video sequence will run to more than a minute or so at most).

2. From the **File** menu, select **Open Movie in New Player ...** In the **Open** dialogue box window, select **Audio files** from the **Files of type** drop down. Navigate to your chosen audio file and click **Open**. *QuickTime* opens a wide range of file types – there is more information on audio files later in this section.

3. The audio file will open in a separate *QuickTime Player* window. To add the music to your video sequence, move the **Selection indicators** along the slider to select an extract of the same length as your video sequence.

An audio file in QuickTime Player *with 40 seconds of music selected*

4. With your music extract highlighted in the slider (see the screenshot above), select **Copy** in the **Edit** menu. You can now close your audio file by selecting **Close** from the **File** menu.

5. In your video sequence, select **Add Scaled** in the **Edit** menu. The **Playback head** will jump to the end of the slider and your music will be added to the video as a background track. Click on the **Go to Start** button to move the **Playback head** to the start of the video and then click on the **Play** button to play your video with its musical accompaniment.

To add text to the video, follow these steps:

1. Open a word processor and type the text that you want to appear on the video.

2. Save your text in the usual way, making sure that it is a *Text only* file – in *Microsoft Word*, for example, select *Plain Text (.txt)* from the **Save as type** drop down, before clicking the **Save** button.

3. With your video sequence open, select **Import** from the **File** menu. Navigate to your saved Text only file in the **Import** dialogue box window. Click to select the file and click on the **Convert** button.

4. You will now be asked where you want the converted file to be saved. In this window, click on the **Options** button before saving. Here you can choose how you want the text to appear on screen, including the font type, text size and colour (see the screenshot p. 103). Make sure that you tick the **Keyed Text** checkbox – this will later superimpose the text over the chosen image in your video sequence. Click the **Save** button when ready.

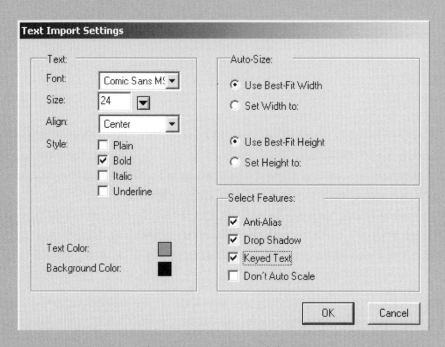

The Text Import Settings *dialogue*

5. The text will now appear in a new *QuickTime Player Pro* window. Select **Copy** from the **Edit** menu. You can now close your text file movie by selecting **Close** from the **File** menu.

6. In your video sequence, use the **Selection indicators** to select the section of the video in which you want the text to appear, e.g. the first 4 seconds for a title.

7. Select **Add Scaled** in the **Edit** menu and the text will appear superimposed over the selected image or images.

As well as getting children to make and record their own music, you can obtain appropriate audio files for this project from a number of sources. Although much maligned because of their synthesised nature, MIDI files are an appropriate option. There are many sites on the Web where you can search for and download free MIDIs

Titles added to a video sequence in QuickTime Player

of classical music, hymns and music from other religions. A good example is www.midisite.co.uk – it has a search engine which allows searches by composer, title or keyword, such as 'Islam'.

You (and possibly children in your class) may be familiar with the MP3 format, used by programs, such as *Winamp*, and portable players, such as the iPod. MP3 is a digital audio compression format. It is designed to greatly reduce the amount of data required to represent audio, yet still sound like a faithful reproduction of the original audio. MP3 music files can be downloaded from many websites – unfortunately, few downloads are free. An exception is Karadar Classical Music World – www.karadar. com – which has a library of 11,000 classical music MP3s, searchable by composer, title or musical genre.

You could, of course, use software, such as *Winamp*, *Real Player* or *iTunes* for Windows or Macintosh, to convert music tracks on CD to MP3 audio files on your computer. The process is very simple. After starting the software, insert a music CD in your computer's CD-ROM drive and the software will almost instantly show the track-listing on screen. To convert a track to an MP3 file on your computer, right click on the title of the track in the listing and then select **Save Track to My Library** (*Real Player*) or **Convert Selection to MP3** (*iTunes*). After a short conversion process, the track will be saved to your computer's hard disk. *Windows Media Player* will also convert CD music tracks, but uses its own proprietary file format (not MP3), which means the music files may not import into your chosen video editing program.

If you choose to use music from CD you must, of course, be careful not to infringe copyright. Use of copyrighted music is permissible in the context of teaching and learning in an educational establishment. The condition is that 'teachers, pupils and others directly connected with the activities' are the only audience that can be involved. It would not be permissible, therefore, to show a video, with a soundtrack derived from a music CD, to an outside audience, such as parents. Full details on copyright restrictions and exceptions, relating to education, are available on the Web at www.intellectual-property.gov.uk.

Transferring children's own performances and compositions to computer as audio files will require sound recording hardware and/or software. This could be as simple a setup as a microphone, plugged into you computer's sound card, and use of *Windows Sound Recorder* (from the **Start** menu, go to **Accessories** > **Entertainment**) to record children's instrumental efforts. Or you could use music-making software, such as *Music Box* from Topologika software (www.topologika.com), to make appropriate soundtracks.

What will the children learn?

The technical skills and understandings children will develop during this project will depend, to an extent, on your chosen video editing package. More sophisticated packages may not, however, lead to the development of more advanced skills – *Windows Movie Maker* and *iMovie* have relatively simple user interfaces, with much of the editing being carried out by drag and drop. A more basic package, such as *QuickTime Player Pro*, will provide greater opportunities for the development of understandings about file types and file management skills. Whatever the package, the project will develop children's visual literacy – specifically, how to convey messages and meaning by the use of images. The subject context should encourage a thoughtful approach to image selection and ordering. A video about a place of worship is not going to benefit from 'flashy' effects and transitions, but will need a sensitive and perceptive choice of apposite images.

Challenging the more able and supporting the less able: modifying the project for older and younger pupils

More experienced pupils may benefit from use of the more sophisticated features of a digital video package – they could explore, for example, the effectiveness of colour washes, monochrome or sepia effects on the video. If a digital video camera is available, pupils could assemble and edit a video, using moving images. All video editing packages will let users order and reorder movie clips – larger images and longer clips will put great demands on your computer memory, however, so it is advisable to use up-to-date, powerful PCs or Macs when setting higher order challenges. Pupils could be challenged to convey an impression of a more unfamiliar or distant place of worship using images from an external source, such as an image library. The SCRAN website (www.scran.ac.uk) has a good selection of images showing the inside and outside of the places of worship of all major religions. If you subscribe to the service, go to **Pathfinder Packs** > **Religion** > **Religions** > **Religious buildings**.

For less experienced or younger pupils, you could pre-prepare and order images and appropriate audio files for assembly into a video sequence. Although children's choices would be more limited, the project would then be accessible to those with less well-developed technical skills. Peer mentoring during the project would also be an effective way of supporting less experienced pupils.

Why teach this?

Visits to places of worship are a key element of the programme of study for KS2 in the QCA national framework for religious education and the QCA religious education scheme of work. The national framework recommends that pupils should 'encounter religion through visitors or visits to places of worship' and should gain experience of 'worship and sacred places: where, how and why people worship'. In Y4, Unit 4D of the scheme of work focuses on a study of religions represented in the school locality. In Y6, Units 6B and 6E are concerned explicitly with visits to places of worship – a mosque and a Christian church. The project provides a means by which such visits could be followed up in a meaningful and motivating way.

The project is a particularly effective way of teaching ICT National Curriculum requirement 3b: 'to be sensitive to the needs of the audience and think carefully about the content and quality when communicating information'. The subject context should encourage a thoughtful and reflective approach to communication. The use of visuals and music should meet the needs of visual and auditory learners. Because of their constant exposure to visual communication through TV, video and film, most children are already familiar with the 'language' of moving images and will find the project an engaging context for articulating their understandings. Research by Reid *et al.* (2002) found that teaching and learning with digital video was effective in a number of ways: it 'increased pupil engagement with the curriculum; promoted and developed a range of learning styles; motivated and engaged a wider range of pupils than traditional teaching methods, so providing greater access to the curriculum.' Qualitative evidence from their study suggests that it 'stimulates and supports the development of other skills, such as problem solving, negotiation, thinking, reasoning and risk-taking' (ibid.).

The project is a particularly effective context for developing children's visual literacy – the ability to communicate by visual means. In an age of increasingly visual communication methods, the development of print literacy is no longer enough. Writing in *The Reading Teacher*, Smolin and Lawless (2003: 578) state:

> In this technological age, teachers must expand their students' technological, visual, and information literacy as well as provide them with a sense of intertextuality, or the ability to make meaning from a variety of texts. This requires teachers to reshape their curricula and enhance students' abilities to understand and use multiple technologies in order to acquire, evaluate, and organize information.

The project engages pupils in communication using images, audio and text, thus providing a learning experience to develop multiple literacies.

See also *Learning ICT with English* Project 4 (*Working with audio*), *Science* Project 8 (*Digital video – free frame*) and *Arts* Project 10 (*Creating a digital a 'silent film'*) for related activities.

References and further reading

Reid, M., Burn, A. and Parker, D. (2002) *Evaluation Report of the Becta Digital Video Pilot Project.* Coventry: Becta.
Available online at www.becta.org.uk/page_documents/research/dvreport_241002.pdf
Smolin, L. and Lawless, K. (2003) 'Becoming literate in the technological age: new responsibilities and tools for teachers', *The Reading Teacher*, 56, March, 570–8.

Index